the **sewing**
workshop

the sewing workshop

learn to sew with 30+ easy,
pattern-free projects

L I N D A   L E E

sixth&spring books
NEW YORK

sixth&spring books

161 Avenue of the Americas

New York, New York 10013

sixthandspringbooks.com

Editorial Director: Joy Aquilino

Senior Editor: Michelle Bredeson

Art Director: Diane Lamphron

Editorial Assistant: Alexandra Joinnides

Instructions Editor: Pat Harste

Designer: Joy Toltzis Makon

Photographer: Dan Howell

Photo Stylist: Laura Maffeo

Illustrators: Matt Dojny and Jane Fay

Vice President, Publisher: Trisha Malcolm

Creative Director: Joe Vior

Production Manager: David Joinnides

President: Art Joinnides

Library of Congress Catalog Control Number: 2011942090

ISBN 978-1-936096-40-4

Manufactured in China

1 3 5 7 9 10 8 6 4 2

First Edition

contents

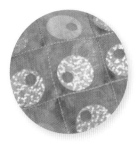

contents

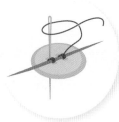

Home Accents

Bags & Totes

Wear It

preface

ACROSS THE COUNTRY,
people are learning to sew and
enjoying their new hobby
to make gifts, save money, or
simply express their creativity.
If you've never sewn before,
this book will help demystify
the process.

SEWING ENCOMPASSES A WIDE RANGE OF TECHNIQUES, from stitching on a button to creating a haute couture evening gown. Those of generations before us sewed because they had to. They had to put clothes on their family's back, utilizing any scrap of fabric they could find, from old overalls to feed sacks. A new piece of fabric was a luxury and used only for the most special occasion.

TODAY, WE NO LONGER "NEED" TO SEW. Fashionable clothes and soft furnishings are available everywhere and for every budget. While professional sewing is still a serious and respected art, home sewing has evolved from a necessity to a fun hobby that's creative, rewarding and relaxing. Sure, you can buy a placemat that kind of goes with your decor. But now, you'll be able to match your decor exactly using beautiful fabrics in colors and textures you choose yourself! And, gifts for family and friends are even more special and appreciated when you make them yourself.

THE SEWING WORKSHOP **GIVES YOU THE KNOWLEDGE** and skills to make you a bona fide sewer. From tools to use and terms to know to the essential techniques—it's all here! Each of the more than thirty fabulous projects introduces you to a new skill or combination of skills to practice; all the while you'll be making super fashions for you and your home. The easy-to-follow, step-by-step directions and clear illustrations ensure success.

THE PROJECTS ARE SPECIFICALLY DESIGNED not only to teach you how to sew, but to inspire your own creativity. Start by making one of the projects according to the directions, then make it again your way! Change the size, make up your own detail, use some outrageous fabric or decorate it with something old that you've had stashed away.

WHATEVER YOU DO, have a blast and be proud of it, because **YOU MADE IT YOURSELF!**

**THIS CHAPTER
OFFERS AN OVERVIEW**
of the basics of the sewing
process—the materials, tools, and
techniques you'll need to make all
the projects in this book—from
preparing fabrics, to pressing, to
creating special elements.

sewing starters

fabric basics

THE ANATOMY OF FABRIC

The woven edge of a fabric is called the **selvage** and runs parallel to the lengthwise grain of fabric. The right-angled edge to the selvage is called the **crosswise grain.**

Fabrics have a right side and a wrong side, and it's important to know which is which before you begin your project. The way the fabric is displayed on the bolt is a good clue to distinguishing the right and wrong sides. Most cottons and linens are placed on the bolt with the right side facing out, while woolens are generally bolted with the right side facing in. For knits, the cut edge usually rolls toward the right side when pulled. Unfortunately, there are no real hard-and-fast rules. So, if you're unsure, either ask the salesperson or use the side that you like the best.

BIAS

This is any diagonal line intersecting the lengthwise and crosswise threads. Fabric that has been cut on the bias has more stretch.

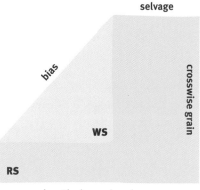

PREPARING YOUR FABRIC

After purchasing your fabric, launder or dry clean it, then press to remove wrinkles and fold marks. See page 40 for information on pressing.

Before laying out and cutting your fabric, you'll need to even off the ends to make them perfectly straight across. These straight edges guide you to the "straight of grain." If the fabric tears easily, simply snip into the selvage and tear off. If not, clip through the selvage and then about $\frac{1}{2}$"/1.3cm into the fabric. Pull on a crosswise thread until the fabric puckers, then cut along the puckered line. Continue to pull and cut across the entire width of fabric. Knits don't tear or have a crosswise thread to pull, so you'll have to even off the ends as best you can using scissors and a yardstick as a guide.

FUSIBLE WEB

This product enables you to adhere two pieces of fabric together using the heat of an iron. Fusible web comes on a heat-resistant paper backing and is sold in packages of sheets or by the yard in various weights. Make sure to use the weight that's closest to the fabric you'll be fusing. See page 41 for details on how to use fusible web for appliqué and other design accents.

fabric basics

ON THE INSIDE

LINING

A lining is a **second layer of fabric** that hides raw seams and other inner construction details. You can use the same fabric or a contrasting fabric. Lining gives a project a professional, finished look. In this book, linings are primarily used in the bag projects.

INTERLINING

Interlining is a separate layer of fabric placed between the lining and the outer fabric. It is cut the same size as the outer fabric. Once it is basted to the outer fabric, **the two layers are treated as one piece.** It is meant to add support or alter the character of the outer fabric. Some good examples of interlining materials are cotton batiste, cotton flannel, lightweight fleece, batting and organza.

UNDERLINING

Underlining is another word for **interlining.**

INTERFACING

Interfacing is used to **shape detail areas and to add body** without adding bulk. Interfacing is available in a wide range of fibers and textures, in either sew-in or fusible varieties. The selection of the appropriate interfacing depends on the weight of the fabric or the end result that you want to achieve. Sew or fuse 4"/10cm squares to the wrong side of your fabric. For fusing methods, follow the manufacturer's instructions included in the packaging. "Handle" the sample from the right side to see how each interfacing looks and feels, then choose the weight you like best.

measuring & marking

WHAT YOU'LL NEED

Here's a list of items you'll need for measuring and laying out your fabric.

TAPE MEASURE

A 60"/150cm flexible cloth or fiberglass tape is essential for measuring both flat and dimensional elements. Find one that has **numbers printed on both sides.**

RULERS

In addition to a yardstick, the most useful measuring tool is a 2" x 18"/ 5 x 46cm **clear plastic ruler** that has a $\frac{1}{8}$"/.3cm grid printed on the front. Use it for measuring and marking and also as a straight edge for cutting with a rotary cutter.

CHALK

A **refillable powdered chalk dispenser** with a wheel marker makes a crisp line and is the perfect companion to a clear plastic ruler.

TRACING WHEEL AND TRANSFER PAPER

Transfer paper works just likes carbon paper, transferring construction markings to fabric with the use of a serrated-edge tracing wheel. The paper is packaged in a mix of colors. **Choose a color close to your fabric color,** yet different enough so that it is still visible. Test the color on scrap fabric first before proceeding.

measuring & marking

MAKING A PATTERN

Most of the projects in this book don't require patterns, but the ones that do (see below, right) use gridded templates that can be copied onto plain paper such as banner paper (comes in a roll and is available at office suppy stores), butcher paper (available at supermarkets) or specialty patternmaking paper (sold in fabric stores). You'll also need a ruler and a pencil.

ENLARGING A PATTERN

On a separate sheet of paper, draw horizontal and vertical lines in a 2"/5cm grid, or make multiple copies of the grid shown opposite and tape them together. Using the pattern templates as a guide, copy each pattern piece line for line to achieve the appropriate scale. Cut along your drawn lines, then use the patterns to make the project.

RETRO BUCKET BAG
page 76

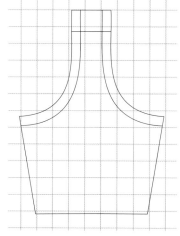

laying out fabric

WHAT YOU'LL NEED

PINS

Glass-head straight pins with good sharp points are a must. To prevent fabric from snagging, replace pins as the points become dull and throw away pins that get bent.

MAGNETIC PIN HOLDER OR PIN CUSHION

Either of these notions is a **handy place to store pins** and keep them accessible.

HOW-TO

Place your washed and pressed fabric on a large, flat surface. Spread it out either in a single layer or, if you're cutting duplicate pieces, folded in half (right sides together) with the selvages perfectly aligned.

If you aren't using a pattern, **roughly measure your project pieces** so you know you have enough fabric, then draw the cutting lines on the fabric using a ruler and chalk marker.

If you're using a pattern, **place your pattern pieces, without pinning,** in a layout that conserves fabric and keeps the pieces on the straight of grain. When your layout is finalized, pin the pattern pieces to the fabric, placing the pins through all layers and perpendicular to the edge of the pattern piece.

WHAT YOU'LL NEED

SCISSORS

A good pair of scissors is essential. **Handles that are slightly angled** help keep the scissors flat on the table without having to lift the fabric too much. Choose an 8"/20.5cm-long pair to cut fabric and a 5"/12.5cm-long pair to trim seams and corners. Both right- and left-handed scissors are available.

ROTARY CUTTER AND CUTTING MAT

This unique cutting system consists of a circular blade attached to a handle that operates like a pizza cutter. It cuts straight edges perfectly when used with a plastic or metal straight-edge ruler and also cuts freehand curves easily. **Rotary cutting requires a special self-healing plastic mat** that will not only protect your work surface but will prevent the rotary cutter blade from getting dull. Choose a large mat that has a 1"/2.5cm grid printed on the front to help make measuring and cutting straight edges accurate.

HOW-TO

Using sharp scissors or a rotary cutter and a cutting mat, cut around each drawn line or pattern piece. Keep one hand on the fabric or the pattern piece as you cut to avoid lifting it from the table too much. Cut with a steady, even motion. Do not cut out a pattern with pinking shears.

sewing with a machine

WHAT YOU'LL NEED

SEWING MACHINE

To make any project in this book, you'll need a basic but reliable machine that sews a **good straight stitch and zigzag stitch.** Read the manual to learn about the different parts of your machine as well as how to thread it correctly.

Besides the standard presser foot, which holds the fabric in place as it's fed through and stitched, there are others you'll need for some of the projects (see opposite).

SERGER

This optional machine trims the fabric and overcasts the edges, all in one stitching motion. It saves times and cleans up the edges of any project, particularly when raw edges are unacceptable. For more information, see page 42.

MACHINE NEEDLES

Needles come in a variety of sizes. Generally, the sheerer the fabric the smaller the needle and the heavier the fabric the larger the needle size required. For example, use a **70/10** needle for **sheer fabric,** an **80/12** for **cotton,** and a **90/14** for **denim or thick wool.** For all the projects in this book you can use a size **80/12 universal** needle. For best results, always begin each new project with a new needle; a used needle can snag the fabric, and fray and break the thread.

THREAD

Thread should be selected in a matching color or one shade darker. Basic choices are **100% cotton** and **polyester.** Always purchase the best threads possible. Cheap threads are prone to breaking and fraying.

PRESSER FEET

ZIPPER FOOT

This narrow presser foot sits to one side of the needle and allows you to sew close to the zipper teeth. It's a **standard accessory** with your sewing machine.

EDGESTITCH FOOT

This extra-accessory foot ensures **straight edgestitching** as the vertical flange of the foot rides along the edge of a fold or seamline.

WALKING FOOT

Another extra-accessory foot that's important to have in your kit is the walking foot. It adds additional feeding and keeps two layers of fabric flowing through the machine at the same rate. This is especially **useful when fabric is slippery** or when you are working with multiple layers.

HEMMER FOOT

A hemmer foot **rolls the fabric into a narrow hem and stitches it** all in one step. There are various widths of hems that can be made from $\frac{1}{16}$"/.2cm to $\frac{1}{4}$"/.6cm.

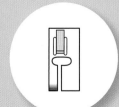

sewing with a machine

MACHINE STITCHES

In addition to the basic straight stitch and zigzag stitch, you'll use these essential stitches and techniques to make the projects.

◀ **BACKSTITCH**

Backstitches **reinforce a stitching line.** To backstitch when machine sewing, begin stitching about $\frac{1}{4}$"/.6cm from the end and sew in reverse to the edge, then stitch forward. Keep stitching to the other end, then reverse your stitches again for about $\frac{1}{4}$"/.6cm.

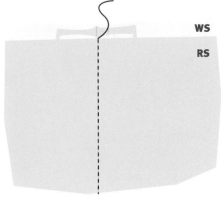

BASTE

A basting stitch is an **elongated stitch used to temporarily** hold two pieces of fabric together.

BAR TACK

This is a zigzag stitch that is sewn with the **feed dogs lowered** so that a few stitches are sewn in the same place.

EDGESTITCH

This is **topstitching** that's placed very close to an edge.

◀ **STITCH IN THE DITCH**

The ditch is the "well" or **center of a seam** that you see on the right side of the fabric. Stitching down the center of the "well" holds layers of fabric together invisibly.

This stitch is **sometimes used as an appliqué stitch.** Begin with the zigzag stitch feature on your sewing machine, then adjust the stitch length so the stitches sew parallel. Also adjust the stitch width to achieve the desired width of the line of satin stitches.

STAYSTITCH

This is a line of stitches **made through only one layer of fabric.** It serves as a guideline for clipping and joining a curve edge to other edges, as well as to prevent the fabric from stretching.

TOPSTITCH

Topstitching emphasizes the structural lines of a project and helps to hold seams and edges in place. This machine stitch is sewn on the right side of the fabric using either **contrasting or matching thread** and is usually done at least $\frac{1}{4}$"/.6cm from an edge.

▼ TIE OFF

When ending your stitching before reaching an edge, and for a **cleaner look without visible backstitching,** pull the bobbin thread to bring the top thread to the wrong side. Tie both thread ends together and clip near the knot.

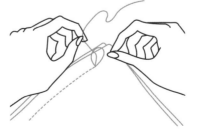

sewing by hand

HAND-SEWING NEEDLES

Crewel embroidery needles have the largest eyes, for easier threading, and the sharpest points as well.

THREAD

You can use the same thread for sewing by hand as you do for machine sewing (see page 20).

HAND-SEWING STITCHES

RUNNING STITCH

The running stitch is a **temporary stitch used for basting** and is intended to be removed. It is done using a contrasting color thread so it's easy to see the stitches when removing them. The running stitch can be stitched either by hand or by machine.

◀ SLIPSTITCH

The slipstitch **joins a folded edge to a flat layer** of fabric. Working from right to left, insert the needle into the folded edge for about $1/4$"/.6cm, then pick up a single thread of the other layer. Insert the needle into the folded edge again and continue as before. This stitch is also used to join two folded edges together such as the opening in a pillow cover.

KNOTTING THE THREAD

There are two choices to end your hand stitches: to take several backstitches or to knot the thread.

1 To knot, begin on the underside of your project. Take the last stitch and pull the thread until a small loop remains.

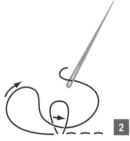

2 Take the needle through the loop, pulling the thread a second time until another small loop is formed.

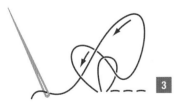

3 Insert the needle through the second loop for the last time and pull the thread taut, forming a small knot at the base of the stitches.

constructing a seam

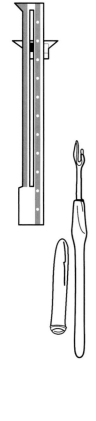

WHAT YOU'LL NEED

SEAM GAUGE

This handy 6"/15cm **metal ruler** has a sliding marker and is used to mark and check small measurements during construction.

SEAM RIPPER

This penlike tool has a **sharp point and a small cutting groove.** It's used to quickly and accurately remove stitches so you can correct mistakes.

SEAMING ESSENTIALS

SEAM ALLOWANCE

There are **three standard seam allowances** that you should know. For **garments,** it's a ⅝"/1.6cm seam allowance. **Home decorating and other craft projects** use a ½"/1.3cm seam, and **quilting** projects traditionally use a ¼"/.6cm allowance. **The seam allowance for all the projects in this book is ½"/1.3cm.**

STITCH LENGTH

Use a stitch length of 2mm to 2.5mm for most fabrics. The general rule is **the heavier the fabric, the longer the stitch length.**

SEWING A SEAM

When pinning the edges of your fabric together, place the pins at right angles to the seamline with the heads toward the raw edges. **Do not sew over pins.** Doing so can alter the timing of your sewing machine and may break your machine needle. Simply remove them as you stitch to them.

Always position the fabric so that the **raw edges are on the right-hand side of the presser foot** and the excess fabric or project is to the left-hand side of the presser foot.

When **sewing a corner,** sew to the turning point and insert the needle into the fabric. Raise the presser foot and pivot the fabric. Lower the presser foot and continue sewing.

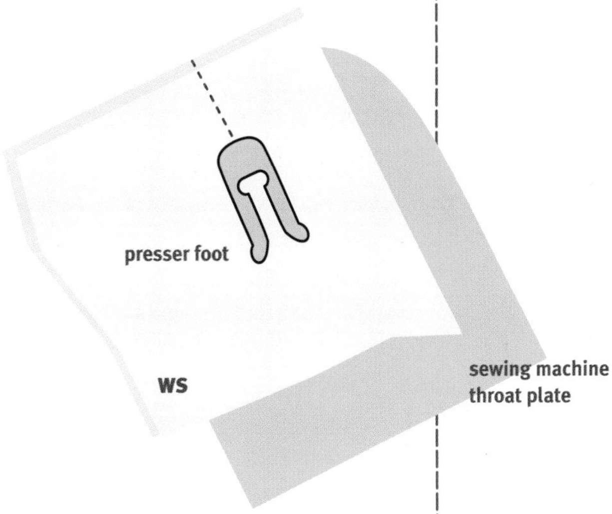

presser foot

WS

sewing machine
throat plate

constructing a seam

POINT TURNER

This small wooden or plastic tool has a point at one end to push out small corners.

PRESSING SEAMS

After sewing a seam, **press the seam open** unless otherwise specified. See pressing how-to's on page 41.

TRIMMING SEAMS AND CORNERS

Trim seam allowances where **less bulk is desired.** In general, exposed seam allowances do not need to be trimmed. Trim enclosed seam allowances to about $1/4$"/.6cm.

For more information about trimming seams, see Finishing on page 42.

For the **corners of an enclosed seam,** trim across the point close to the seam. Then trim diagonally along either side of the point to eliminate bulk when the corner is turned.

SPECIAL SEAMS

▼ DOUBLE-STITCHED SEAM

This seam is especially **suited to knits** and other stretch fabrics. Stitch a plain seam, then zigzag stitch again ⅛"/.3cm from the first seam. Trim the seam allowance close to the stitching.

▶ FRENCH SEAM

This seam finish **encloses the seam allowance** and gives a very neat appearance. It looks like a plain seam on the right side and a small, neat tuck on the wrong side.

1 Pin the wrong sides together and stitch ¼"/.6cm from the raw edge. Trim the seam allowance to about ⅛"/.3cm.

2 With the right sides together, crease along the stitched seam, encasing the raw edges. Then stitch a ⅜"/1cm seam. Press the seam to one side.

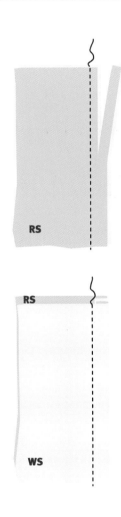

RS

RS

WS

constructing a seam

INSERTING A ZIPPER

Sew the seam, basting the portion where the zipper will be installed. Press the seam open. Center the right side of the zipper teeth over the seam on the **wrong side** of the fabric. Hand baste in place along the outer edges of the zipper tape. **Using a zipper foot,** topstitch $1/4$"/.6cm on each side of the seam and across the bottom.

ZIPPERED POUCH
page 58

The size of a buttonhole is determined by the size of the button. To determine the width (or size) of the buttonhole needed, measure the diameter of the button and then the thickness. Add these two measurements together, then add another $\frac{1}{8}$"/.3cm. Following the instructions in your sewing machine manual, **make a test buttonhole first.** For best results, use scrap fabric from the project, making sure to have the same amount of fabric layers as the project. Cut the buttonhole open using the appropriate tool, such as a chisel-type buttonhole cutter and wood block (see below for details). Test-fit the button in the buttonhole. Make adjustments to the width if necessary.

When you're ready to add buttonholes to the project, be sure to mark the beginning and end of each on the fabric with **chalk lines** to ensure proper placement.

BUTTONHOLE CUTTER

This important gadget is simply a beveled blade attached to a wooden handle. It's used to slice through the center of a buttonhole without cutting the buttonhole threads. To use it safely, **place a small block of wood** underneath the buttonhole before cutting.

sewing a hem

Precision hems can be accomplished when using a **pressing template.** Cut strips of tag board (from a manila file folder) in $1/4$"/.6cm increments and from 1"/2.5cm to 2"/5cm wide.

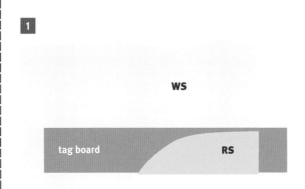

1

WS

tag board   RS

1 To make a $1\frac{1}{4}$"/3cm finished hem with a $\frac{1}{2}$"/1.3cm turn down, place a $1\frac{3}{4}$"/4.5cm tag board template on the wrong side of the fabric about $1\frac{3}{4}$"/4.5cm from the raw edge. Bring the hem allowance up and over the template, matching the raw edge of the fabric with the top edge of the template. Press in place.

2 Place a 1¼"/3cm template in the creaseline and press ½"/1.3cm over the bottom of the template.

3 Press the folded hem in place. Hand baste along the inner fold.

4 On the right side of the fabric, draw a chalk line next to the basting stitches and topstitch the hem in place.

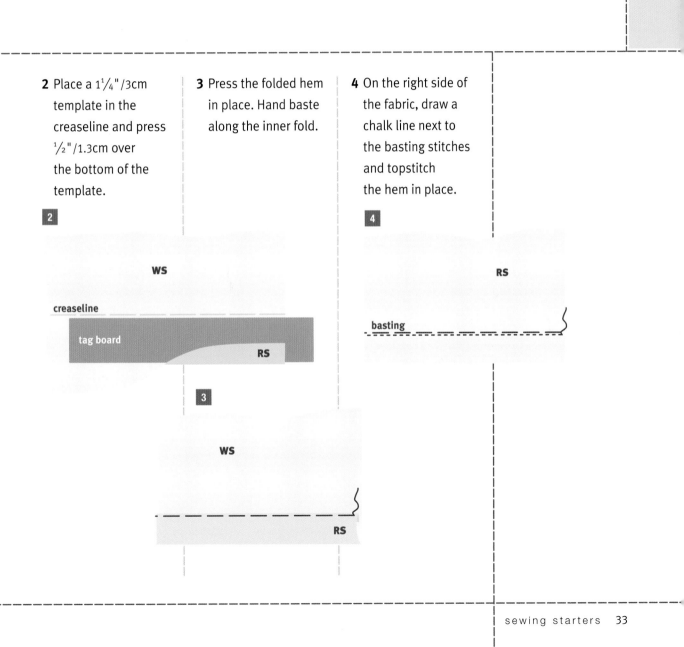

special elements

FABRIC TUBES, FOLDED STRAPS & DRAWSTRINGS

Fabric tubes and folded straps are used interchangeably for either bag handles and straps, or drawstrings. Fabric tubes don't have visible stitching, while folded straps have stitching that shows on both edges.

Detail of
SWING SATCHEL
page 82

HOW-TO

FABRIC TUBE

Cut a piece of fabric 1"/2.5cm wide by the desired length. Fold the strip in half lengthwise with the right sides together. Stitch the length of the strip ½"/1.3cm from the folded edge, forming a tube. Insert the **ball end of a metal bodkin** (see opposite) into one end of the tube. Hand sew the eye of the bodkin to the fabric for 3 or 4 stitches, then wrap the thread around the end a few times and knot. Push the ball end of the bodkin through the tube, forcing the sewn end to disappear into the tube. Continue to push the bodkin through until the tube has been turned to the right side.

FOLDED STRAP

Cut the strap piece the size indicated in the bag preparation. Fold the strip in half lengthwise with the wrong sides together. Fold each raw edge to the center crease and press. **(See prairie points how-to step 1 on page 39.)** Edgestitch the outer edges of the folded strip. **(See prairie points how-to step 2 on page 39).**

DRAWSTRING

Cut a piece of fabric 1"/2.5cm wide by the desired length. Fold the strip in half lengthwise with the right sides together. Stitch the length of the strip $^1/_2$"/1.3cm from the folded edge, forming a tube. Insert the **ball end of a metal bodkin** (see right) into one end of the tube. Hand sew the eye of the bodkin to the fabric for 3 or 4 stitches, then wrap the thread around the end a few times and knot. Push the ball end of the bodkin through the tube, forcing the sewn end to disappear into the tube. Continue to push the bodkin through until the tube has been turned to the right side.

BODKIN

This curious little metal tool makes it possible to turn narrow strips of stitched fabric, such as a drawstring, to the right side. It measures 6"/15cm long and has an eye at one end and a small ball at the other end.

special elements

DRAWSTRING CASING

A drawstring can be led through an inside casing by way of an **in-seam opening.** Simply leave an opening in the seam the width of the drawstring. Attach a large safety pin to the end of the drawstring. Being careful not to twist the drawstring, work the pin through the casing and out the same opening.

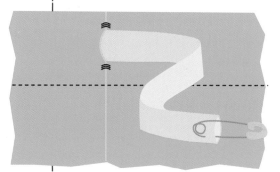

CONTINUOUS DRAWSTRING

The technique for making a continuous drawstring is best used with the **folded fabric method.** After feeding the drawstring through the casing, remove a few stitches along the edges and sew the ends of the drawstring together in a small seam. Press the seam open, refold the fabric and complete the edgestitching.

POCKET

Cut the pocket piece according the bag preparation instructions. Finish the top edge of the pocket. Turn the top hem allowance to the wrong side of the pocket and topstitch. Press the remaining seam allowances to the wrong side using the pressing directions for hems described on page 33. Pin the pocket to the bag or lining. Edgestitch the side and bottom edges, **reinforcing the stitches** at the upper ends.

KNOTTED BUTTONS

Strips of fabric can be **folded and knotted** to create clever buttons.

1 Using strips of fabric cut $1^3/_4$" x $8^1/_2$" / 4.5 x 21.5cm, fold each strip in half lengthwise with the wrong sides together. Press. Fold each raw edge to the center crease. Do not press.

2 Tie a loose knot in the center of the strip. To beef up the knot, pull one end of the strip through the knot again.

3 Tie one more knot onto the first knot.

Detail of
CONNECTING SCARVES
page 120

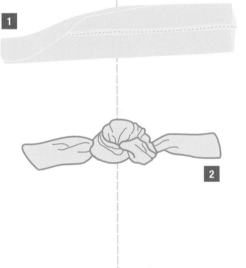

special elements

PRAIRIE POINTS

A prairie point is a decorative and novel way to make a **loop buttonhole.**

creaseline ··································· RS

RS

WS

1 Cut a strip of fabric 2"/5cm wide by about 4"/10cm. Fold the strip in half lengthwise with the wrong sides together. Fold each raw edge to the center crease.

Detail of **JOURNAL COVER** *page 56*

2 Edgestitch the outer edges of the folded strip.

3 On a pressing surface, hold one end of the strip with one hand. With the other hand, fold the opposite end down at a right angle, creating a diagonal fold. Press.

4 Bring the other end down and at a right angle. Press. Trim the length of the prairie point to the size of the button and include a seam allowance.

RS

pressing

IRON

A good steam/dry iron is an essential piece of equipment. Seasoned sewers prefer an iron that **does not have an automatic turn-off.**

PRESSING SURFACE

Pressing is best accomplished over a cotton-covered surface padded with a thick felt pad, wool blanket, cotton batting or a commercially prepared ironing board pad. It's best to **avoid silver-coated silicone surfaces.**

SLEEVE BOARD

Use this double-sided ironing board to **press small areas** or **tubular pieces.**

PRESS CLOTH

Some fabrics, such as woolens, will take on a shine when they come in contact with the hot metal plate of an iron. To prevent this problem, **cover the area to be pressed with a press cloth.** You can purchase one, or you can use an old cotton or linen dish towel.

IRON CLEANER

It is important to use a **paste iron cleaner** regularly to keep the sole of the iron clean and smooth.

HOW-TO

Press during **each stage of construction** so that only a light pressing will be needed when the project is completed.

STEAM

The hot moisture of a steam iron provides just enough water vapor to get truly flat seams and edges. **Use a press cloth** to prevent shine and to protect the fabric from too much heat.

SEAMS

Pressing seams is done in two steps. First "meld" the seam by pressing the stitching line flat to blend the stitches into the fabric. Now separate the two seam edges to "open" the seam, then press flat. This is called to **"press open."**

FUSING

Cut the accent fabric to be fused at least 1"/2.5cm larger all around than the size of the piece of fusible web. To fuse, place the web, web side down, on the wrong side of the accent fabric. Using a medium-hot dry iron, press to adhere. When cool, peel away the paper backing. Position the accent fabric, fused side down, on the right side of the background fabric and press to adhere in place.

APPLIQUÉ

Appliqué techniques are used to apply a separate piece of fabric as a **decoration or trim** to a background. Fuse fusible web (see above and page 13) to the wrong side of the decorative piece of fabric and iron it onto the project. Adjust your zigzag stitch width to a fairly closed satin stitch. Begin sewing in the center of a straight line, positioning the stitch to cover the raw edge. Insert the needle at a corner, raise the presser foot, and pivot the fabric. Lower the presser foot and continue sewing until all edges are covered. At the last stitch, leave thread tails when removing the project from the sewing machine. Pull the bottom thread to pull the top thread to the underside. Tie the threads in a knot to secure.

finishing

Projects look more professional when seams and edges are finished. Finishing helps prevent raveling and ensures durability. There are several methods to choose from.

WHAT YOU'LL NEED

PINKING SHEARS

These unique scissors have **zigzag-shaped blades** and are used to finish the raw edges of fabric to prevent fraying.

FINISHING SEAMS

PINKED

Trimming the edge of a fabric with pinking shears is the **simplest and flattest** seam finish. For an even more secure finish, stitch $\frac{1}{4}$"/.6cm from each edge before you begin to pink.

TURNED AND STITCHED

After a seam has been sewn and pressed open, **turn under the raw edges** of the seam allowances and stitch close to the edge.

SERGED SEAMS

The serger evens and overcasts the edge of the fabric to prevent raveling. It looks exactly like ready-to-wear or other purchased items made from fabric. See serger on page 20.

TWO-THREAD ROLL HEM

This is an adjusted stitch on a serger that utilizes one needle thread and the lower looper thread to roll and finish edges of fabric.

THREE-THREAD ROLL HEM

This is an adjusted stitch on a serger that utilizes one needle thread and the upper and lower looper threads to roll and finish edges of fabric.

SEWING ON A BUTTON

Buttons are available as either the **sew-through** or **shank** variety. For either type, thread a needle, double the strand, then knot the ends together.

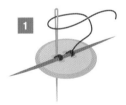

1 For a **sew-through button,** take one stitch through the right side of the fabric and insert the needle through one hole in the button. Place a **toothpick** on top of the button between the holes. Take the needle down through the other hole and take another stitch in the fabric. Repeat for several stitches ending with the thread under the button.

2 Remove the toothpick and raise the button to the top of the stitches. Wind the thread tightly under the button to form a shank. Secure the thread on the right side with several small stitches close to the shank.

Attach a **shank button** with small stitches sewn through the shank. Secure the thread on the right side of the fabric with several small stitches close to the shank.

EVEN IF YOU'RE AN ABSOLUTE BEGINNER, the nine stylish projects in this chapter make decorating and organizing your home—and giving creative wedding or housewarming gifts with a personal touch— simple and easy.

home accents

appliqué placemat

Create a colorful self-lined placemat that's made using three mix-and-match cotton fabrics.
This easy iron-on appliqué technique gives the look of patchwork but without the hassle.

SIZE
13" x 18"/33 x 45.5cm

MATERIALS
- 1³/₄yd/1.75m of fabric **A** for top and bottom
- ¹/₂yd/.5m of fabric **B** for center accent
- ¹/₈yd/.3m of fabric **C** for trim
- ¹/₂yd/.5m of fusible web
- Thread

TECHNIQUES
Appliqué, *page 41*

Fusing, *page 41*

Slipstitch, *page 24*

Trimming a corner, *page 28*

PREPARATION
- Cut **two** pieces of **fabric A** 14" x 19"/35.5 x 48cm.

- Fuse fusible web to the wrong side of fabric **B.**

- Cut **one** piece of **fabric B** 9" x 14"/23 x 35.5cm.

- Fuse fusible web to the wrong side of fabric **C.**

- Cut **two** pieces of **fabric C** ¹/₂" x 15"/1.3 x 38cm.

- Cut **two** pieces of **fabric C** ¹/₂" x 10"/1.3 x 25.5cm.

CONSTRUCTION

1 **Center fabric B** on right side of one piece of fabric **A** and press to fuse.

2 **Fuse C trim strips** over the raw edges of the center accent. Using a zigzag stitch and starting along one edge, appliqué the trim strips to the fabric. Stitch along both raw edges of the trim strips.

3 **With right sides together,** sew the top of the placemat to the bottom, leaving an opening along one edge. Trim the corners.

4 **Turn the placemat to the outside.** Press the edges, then slipstitch the opening closed. ✳

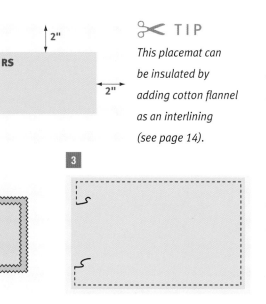

✂ **TIP**

This placemat can be insulated by adding cotton flannel as an interlining (see page 14).

trimmed napkin

This charming napkin is the perfect companion to the appliquéd placemat. Here you'll learn how to add trim to conceal a raw edge. Choose a fabric and trim that are both washable.

SIZE
16" x 16"/40.5cm

MATERIALS
- 1yd/1m of fabric
- 8yd/7.5m of trim
- Washable glue stick
- Thread

TECHNIQUES
Pressing with a template (see Sewing a Hem), *page 32*

PREPARATION
- Cut **four** pieces of **fabric** 16½" x 16½"/42cm.

CONSTRUCTION

1 **Press** ¼"/.6cm to the right side of all four edges.

2 **Starting in the center of one edge,** lightly glue the trim to the right side of the napkin, covering the raw edge of the fabric with the trim. As you go around the napkin, turn each corner at a 90° angle, by overlapping the trim to create a diagonal fold. To end, overlap the trim over the starting point. Stitch the trim to the napkin. ✳

✂ TIPS

- *An easy way to cut a perfect square is to tear the fabric rather than cutting with scissors. Snip into the edges of the fabric and tear in both directions.*
- *If your fabric does not tear easily, mark exact cutting lines using an "L" square.*
- *A good source for retro cotton fabrics is resale shops that sell vintage clothing.*
- *Rickrack is an interesting alternative to ribbon trim.*

layered table runner

Have fun with fabrics while making an elegant table topper. Here we use a handsome Chinese brocade to finish the ends with extra-wide borders.

FINISHED SIZE
14" x 62"/35.5 x 150cm

MATERIALS
- ½yd/.5m of sheer fabric **A**
- ½yd/.5m of sheer fabric **B**
- ½yd/.5m of brocade fabric
- Thread

TECHNIQUES
Slipstitch, *page 24*

Here, two contrasting colors of sheer organza are layered in a clever way to give the illusion of three different shades.

PREPARATION
- Cut **one** piece of **sheer fabric A** 15" x 45"/38 x 114.5cm.

- Cut **one** piece of **sheer fabric B** 15" x 45"/38 x 114.5cm.

- Cut **two** pieces of **brocade fabric** 15" x 19"/38 x 48cm.

CONSTRUCTION

1 **With right sides together,** stitch the long edges together of sheer fabric A and sheer fabric B. Trim the seams to ¼"/.5cm and press open. Turn to the right side.

2 **Refold the tube** so that the seams are 3½"/9cm from each fold.

3 **Press** ½"/1.3cm to the wrong side of one short end of each brocade fabric piece.

4 **With right sides together,** stitch the unpressed end of the brocade to one end of the sheer tube. Press the seam toward the brocade. Repeat for the other end.

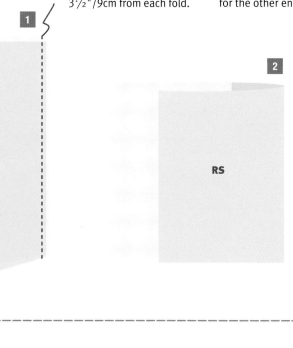

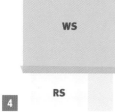

5 With right sides together, fold the brocade back on itself, leaving the ½"/1.3cm turned back. Stitch the side seams and trim. Press the seams open and turn to the outside.

6 Slipstitch the folded edge of the brocade to the stitching line of the sheer fabrics. ✳

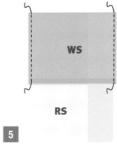

fringed pillow

Stitch up your first pillow in a fun retro-print fabric that's trimmed with playful ball fringe. The basics of this project will introduce you to pillow-making of all types.

SIZE
18" x 18"/45.5cm

MATERIALS
- ²⁄₃yd/.5m of fabric
- 2¹⁄₈yd/2m of ball fringe
- 18" x 18"/45.5cm pillow form
- Thread

TECHNIQUES
Backstitch, *page 22*

Slipstitch, *page 24*

Zipper foot (see Presser Feet), *page 21*

✂ TIP

Stitch on the side of the pillow on which you can see the previous stitches, and stitch just next to those stitches toward the center of the pillow.

PREPARATION
- Cut **two** pieces of **fabric** 19" x 19"/48 x 48cm.

CONSTRUCTION

1 **Starting in the center of one edge,** pin the flange of the ball fringe trim to the right side of the pillow front. Using a zipper foot, begin stitching the flange to the pillow.

2 **At the corner,** insert the needle into the fabric and clip the flange to the needle. Pivot the pillow and continue sewing along each side. Overlap the flange to end.

3 **With the right sides together,** sew the pillow back to the front, leaving about a 12"/30cm opening. Backstitch at the beginning and end.

4 **Turn the pillow to the outside.** Insert the pillow form.

5 **Slipstitch** the opening closed. ✳

RS

WS

quilted throw

This machine-quilted throw uses two contrasting colors of luxurious nubby silk douppioni and is interlined with cozy cotton flannel.

FINISHED SIZE
45" x 60"/114.5 x 152.5cm

MATERIALS
- 1²/₃yd/1.6m each of two colors silk douppioni
- 1²/₃yd/1.6m of cotton flannel
- Chalk marker
- Long straight edge
- Safety pins
- Quilt basting spray
- Thread

TECHNIQUES
Interlining (see On the Inside), *page 14*

Slipstitch, *page 24*

Topstitch, *page 23*

Trimming a corner, *page 28*

Walking foot (see Presser Feet), *page 21*

PREPARATION
- Use the **width of the douppioni fabrics** as the project width.

- **Spray fabrics with quilt basting** according to label directions. Quilt basting spray will prevent the fabrics from shifting as you sew them together.

- **Stack the three fabrics** in the following order starting on the bottom:

    One color of silk douppioni **right-side up**

    Second color of silk douppioni **right-side down**

    Cotton flannel

- Trim the fabrics so that they are all the same size; approximately 60"/152.5cm long.

- Pin the layers together along all four edges.

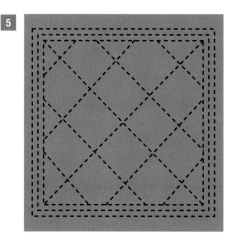

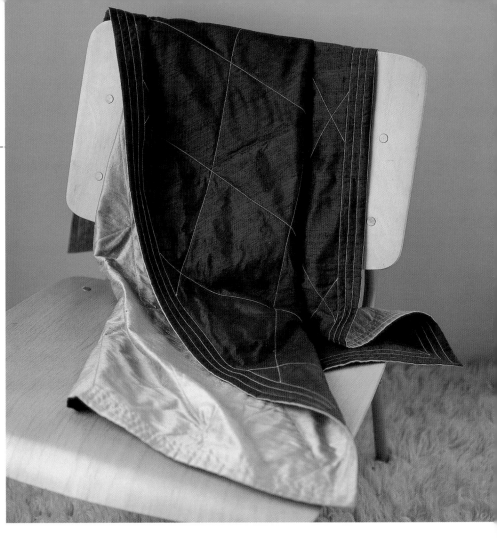

CONSTRUCTION

1 **Using the standard presser foot,** stitch around all edges of the throw, leaving about a 12"/30.5cm opening along one edge. Trim the corners, turn the work to the outside and press the edges.

2 **Slipstitch** the opening closed.

3 **Using safety pins,** pin about every 6"/15cm over the entire throw.

4 **Sew three parallel lines** about ½"/1.3cm apart around the edges.

5 **Using a chalk marker,** draw parallel lines 6"/15cm apart diagonally across the throw, starting and ending the first line from corner to corner.

6 **Starting at the center line** and moving toward the edges, stitch the marked lines using the **walking foot.** Use the same color thread for both sides. Backstitch at each end. ✳

journal cover

This charming cover features a handy patch pocket that's accented with a prairie point button loop closure. Handles add a fun touch and make it easy to tote.

SIZE

This cover fits over a 5½" x 8¼"/14 x 21cm 76-page spiral-bound sketchbook

MATERIALS

- ½yd/.5m of fabric
- ⅛yd/.25m of ½"/13mm-wide ribbon
- ⅝"/16mm button
- Thread
- 5½" x 8¼"/ 14 x 21cm spiral-bound sketchbook

TECHNIQUES

Edgestitch, *page 22*

Prairie points, *page 38*

Running stitch, *page 24*

Sewing on a button, *page 43*

Topstitch, *page 23*

Trimming a corner, *page 28*

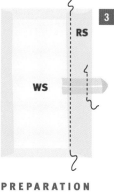

PREPARATION

- Cut **one** piece of **fabric** 10" x 15"/25.5 x 38cm for body.

- Cut **two** pieces of **fabric** 10" x 4½"/25.5 x 11.5cm for flaps.

- Cut **two** pieces of **fabric** 3" x 11"/7.5 x 28cm for handles.

- Cut **one** piece of **fabric** 6" x 8½"/15 x 21.5cm for pocket.

- Cut **ribbon** 5"/12.5cm long.

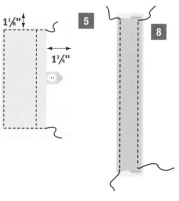

CONSTRUCTION

POCKET

1 **Press** ½"/1.3cm to the wrong side on all edges.

2 **Press** 1"/2.5cm to the wrong side on one long edge.

3 **Make a prairie point button loop** (see page 38) and pin to the wrong side of the pocket hem.

4 **Topstitch the hem,** catching the button loop. Edgestitch the button loop in place at the outer edge.

5 **Pin the pocket** to the right side of the cover 1¾"/4.5cm from the right edge and centering from top to bottom. Edgestitch three sides of the pocket.

6 **Sew the button** under the button loop.

HANDLES

7 **Press** ½"/1.3cm to the wrong side of the long edges of both handle pieces.

8 **With wrong sides together,** fold the handles in half lengthwise. Edgestitch both edges.

9 **Pin handles to both side edges** 2"/5cm from the top and bottom. Baste in place.

FLAPS

10 **Press one long edge** to the wrong side of each flap and edgestitch.

11 **With right sides together,** sew the flaps to each side of the body on three edges, leaving the edges toward the center free.

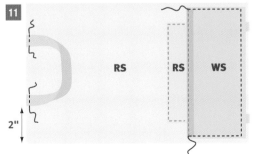

12 **Trim the corners** and turn the flaps to the wrong side. Press the top edges to the wrong side and edgestitch if necessary.

13 **Insert** the journal. ✳

zippered pouch

This handy little pouch has three zipper compartments to keep your jewelry organized. It also does double duty as nifty storage for makeup.

SIZE
8" x 12"/20.5 x 30.5cm

MATERIALS
- ½yd/.5m of fabric
- Three 12"/30.5cm-long medium-weight separating zippers
- Thread

TECHNIQUES
Inserting a zipper, *page 30*

Topstitch, *page 23*

Zipper foot
(see Presser Feet), *page 21*

PREPARATION
- Cut **one** piece of **fabric** 9" x 19"/23 x 48cm for piece **A.**

- Cut **two** pieces of **fabric** 9" x 3½"/23 x 9cm for pieces **B** and **C.**

CONSTRUCTION

1 **Press** ½"/1.3cm to the wrong side of the short ends of piece **A** and both long sides of pieces **B** and **C.**

2 **Starting at the bottom zipper,** place the top folded edge of piece **A** next to the zipper teeth, centering the zipper across the width. Using a zipper foot, stitch next to the fold through the seam and zipper tape.

3 **Place the bottom folded edge** of piece **B** on the other side of the zipper teeth. Stitch next to the fold through the seam and zipper tape.

4 **Stitch top folded edge** of piece **B** to a second zipper. Stitch zipper to bottom edge of piece **C.**

5 **Stitch top edge** of piece **C** to zipper.

6 **Stitch top edge** of piece **A** to the top of third zipper, forming a tube.

RS

2

RS

7 **Turn the tube** so that the right sides are together and the top zipper teeth are 1"/2.5cm from the top fold. Move the zipper pulls to about the center of the bag. Pin the zipper at the side so that the teeth just meet. Sew both sides, hand walking the presser foot over the zipper teeth.

8 **Trim the excess zipper teeth** and tape even with the sides of the bag.

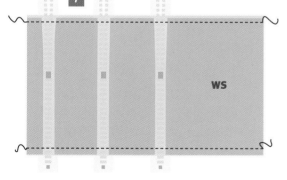

9 **Reaching through one zipper opening,** turn the bag to the outside. Topstitch above the zipper teeth on the two bottom zippers through all layers to form separate compartments. ✳

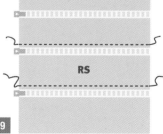

laundry bag

A laundry bag, a linen bag, a drawstring bag, a sack—it's whatever you want it to be. It's an easy bag to make large for toting stuff or small and dressed up for evening.

FINISHED SIZE
20" x 28"/51 x 71cm

MATERIALS
- Two towels 21" x 28"/ 53.5 x 71cm or 1⁷⁄₈yd/ 1.75m fabric for bag
- ¼yd/.25m contrasting fabric for casing and drawstrings
- ²⁄₃yd/.75m lace trim

TECHNIQUES
Baste, *page 22*

Continuous drawstring, *page 36*

Edgestitch, *page 22*

Finishing, *page 42*

Topstitch, *page 23*

PREPARATION
- If using towels, remove hem stitches and press flat, or cut **two** bag pieces 22"/56cm wide x 29"/73.5cm long.

- Cut **two** contrasting pieces 2½"/6.5cm wide x 22"/56cm long for casing.

- Cut enough strips of 1½"/ 4cm wide **contrasting fabric** to sew together to make **two** strips 54"/137cm long.

- Cut **one** piece **lace** 22"/56cm wide.

- Cut **two** strips of **lining** fabric the width of the top of the bag plus seam allowances x 4"/10cm.

CONSTRUCTION

1 **Turn the edges** of each end of the lace to the wrong side and stitch to finish.

2 **Finish the bottom edges** of each bag piece.

3 **Center the lace piece** on the right side of one bag piece, placing the decorative edge of the lace toward the center of the bag. Baste in place.

4 **With right sides together,** sew the sides and bottom of the bag pieces together.

5 **Finish the top edge** of the bag. Fold the top to the wrong side 3½"/9cm. Topstitch near the finished edge of the turndown.

6 **Press the two long edges** of casing strip ½"/1.3cm to the wrong side. Press each end ½"/1.3cm to the wrong side. Pin a casing strip to the right side of both the front and back of the bag 2¾"/7cm from the top and

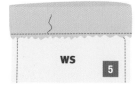

leaving the ends open at the side seams of the bag. Edgestitch both long edges of the casing.

7 **Make two** 54"/137cm long drawstrings. Attach the safety pin to the end of one drawstring. Starting at one side, feed the pin and drawstring through the casing, bringing it out the same side it was inserted.

8 **Feed the second drawstring** through the casing, starting on the side opposite from the previous drawstring and bringing it out on the side of insertion.

9 **Complete each drawstring** as a continuous piece. Loosely knot each drawstring. ✳

lingerie bag

This small bag is perfect for packing and storing delicates. The handle feeds through a loop to create its pouch shape, and a ribbon rosette embellishment adds a frilly touch.

FINISHED SIZE
8"/20.5cm wide x
5½"/14cm high x
4"/10cm deep
(excluding handle)

MATERIALS
- ¼yd/.25m fabric for bag
- ¼yd/.25m lining
- One 9"/23cm zipper
- 1yd/1m of 1½"/38mm-wide ombre taffeta ribbon
- Hand-sewing needle
- Polyester thread

TECHNIQUES
Lining (see On the Inside), *page 14*

Fabric tube, *page 34*

Running stitch, *page 24*

Slipstitch, *page 24*

Zipper foot
(see Presser Feet), *page 21*

PREPARATION
- Cut **one** piece **fabric** 10" x 9"/25.5 x 23cm.

- Cut **one** piece **lining** 10" x 9"/25.5 x 23cm.

- Cut 2"/5cm squares out of each bottom corner of the bag and lining pieces.

- Cut **one** piece 2½" x 13"/6.5 x 33cm for the handle.

- Cut **one** piece 2½" x 4"/6.5 x 10cm for the loop.

CONSTRUCTION

1 **Make fabric tubes** using the handle and loop pieces. The finished width should be ³/₄"/2cm.

2 **With right sides together,** sew both side seams of the bag together. Press open.

3 **Fold the handle and loop tubes** in half and pin one to the right side of each bag side seam. Baste.

4 **Clip** ½"/1.3cm into the seam allowance on both sides of each loop.

5 **With the zipper open** and the zipper pull facing down, center the zipper teeth of one open end of the zipper tape over the handle. The outer edge of the zipper will be about ¼"/.6cm from the raw edge. Begin stitching at the clip and sew the zipper tape to one top edge. At the opposite clip, pivot the stitching and sew across the end of the zipper for ³/₄"/2cm, catching the small

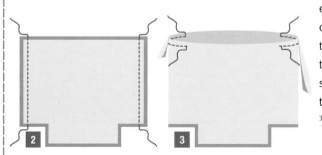

lingerie bag

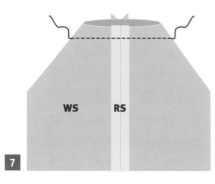

WS RS

7

loop. Pivot at the next clip and stitch the other side of the zipper to the bag. Stitch across the final end.

6 **Stitch the bottom** of the bag together. Press seam open.

7 **With right sides together,** pin the bottom seam and each side seam together at the bottom corners. Stitch a ½"/1.3cm seam allowance. Turn the bag to the outside.

8 **Construct the bag lining** in the same manner as the bag without installing the zipper.

9 **Fold** ½"/1.3cm of the top edge to the wrong side. Insert the lining inside the bag. Slipstitch the lining to the zipper tape.

10 **Make one ribbon rosette** (see instructions at right). Hand tack to the handle side of the bag. ✳

✂ RIBBON ROSETTE

1 Thread a strand of polyester thread into the hand-sewing needle and knot one end.

2 Sew running stitches along the outside edge of the length of the ribbon.

3 Draw up the ribbon, arranging it in concentric circles to look like a flower.

4 Hand tack bottom edges together to hold in place.

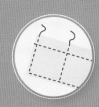

THIS CHAPTER OFFERS TEN TRENDY PROJECTS for carrying everything you need—not just the usual day-to-day items, but groceries, laptops, books, and more—so you can express your style while toting your stuff around town.

bags & totes

flat shopper

Two trimmed tea towels easily make this handy tote that folds flat to store in another bag. Bring it out for an extra shopping bag or a fun fashion accessory.

FINISHED SIZE
16"/40.5cm wide x
19"/48cm tall
(excluding handles)

MATERIALS
- Two embroidered or appliquéd tea towels or ²⁄₃yd/.75m fabric
- Contrasting buttonhole thread

TECHNIQUES
Bar tack, *page 22*

Folded strap, *page 35*

Finishing, *page 42*

Selvage (see Fabric Basics), *page 12*

Tie off, *page 23*

PREPARATION
- Cut **one** piece of **towel or fabric** 33" x 24"/84 x 61cm for the bag, preserving the selvage along one long edge.

- When using towels with striped borders, reserve two lengths of stripes from one towel to use as handles. Use other parts of one towel to piece as necessary to make the bag.

- Cut **two** stripe lengths 24½"/62cm and add seam allowances on the long edges.

CONSTRUCTION

1 **Fold the bag in half** with the right sides together, sew the bottom and side edges of the bag together. Sew a 2"/5cm diagonal line across each bottom corner. Finish the edges.

2 **Turn the top edge** 4½"/11.5cm to the right side and press.

3 **Make two handles** 24½"/62cm long. Finish each end.

4 **Fold under** 1"/1.3cm at each end of the handles. Pin one handle to each side of the bag, placing the ends 2"/5cm from the top and 4"/10cm from each side edge.

5 **Using contrasting buttonhole thread,** bar tack the handle to each bag side in three places. Tie off each thread tail on the inside of the bag. ✳

raw-edge tote

Four pieces of fabric—two for the bag, two for the lining—are stacked and sewn together, leaving the edges unfinished. Purchased straps make this bag sturdy and easy to construct.

FINISHED SIZE

18"/45.5cm wide x 17"/43cm high (excluding straps)

MATERIALS

- ²/₃yd/.75m fabric for bag
- ²/₃yd/.75m lining
- 3yd/2.75m cotton strapping
- Pattern paper

TECHNIQUES

Baste, *page 22*

Edgestitch, *page 22*

Lining (see On the Inside), *page 14*

Pocket, *page 36*

Topstitch, *page 23*

PREPARATION

- Make a paper pattern. Draw a trapezoid shape on the paper 16"/40.5cm across the top, 18"/45.5cm across the bottom and 17"/43cm high. Curve the bottom corners.

- Using the paper pattern, cut **two bag** pieces and **two lining** pieces.

- Cut **one** pocket piece 9¹/₂" x 12"/24 x 30.5cm.

- Cut **two** straps 49"/124.5cm long each.

CONSTRUCTION

1 **Make one pocket** finished size 8¹/₂" x 10¹/₂"/21.5 x 26.5cm.

2 **Center the pocket** on one lining piece, 4¹/₂"/11.5cm below the top raw edge. Edgestitch to the lining.

3 **With wrong sides together,** baste one lining piece to each bag piece.

4 **Press** ¹/₂"/1.3cm to the wrong side of each top edge. Press another 1"/2.5cm to make a 1"/2.5cm finished hem. Topstitch along the inner fold.

5 **Pin one strap** to each bag front, extending the end of the straps 12"/30cm below the top and 3¹/₂"/9cm toward the center at the top hem edge. Topstitch a rectangle to attach the strap to the bag, then reinforce by sewing an "X" through the rectangle as shown. Knot each end of each strap and fringe the ends.

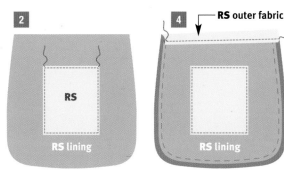

6
With wrong sides together, sew the two bag pieces together, leaving an opening at the top and the side and bottom edges unfinished. ✳

5

RS bag

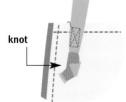

knot

handy shoulder bag

Function meets fashion when you stitch up a handy tote in a fabric that coordinates with your wardrobe. Finish it perfectly with a contrasting fabric lining.

FINISHED SIZE
11" x 13" x
3³/₄"/28 x 33 x 9.5cm
(not including handles)

MATERIALS
- ¹/₂yd/.5m of fabric for outer tote
- ¹/₂yd/.5m of fabric for lining
- ¹/₄yd/.25m of fabric for pocket
- 3yd/3m of 1"/25mm-wide poly/web strapping
- Clear template plastic or lightweight cardboard
- Thread

TECHNIQUES
Edgestitch, *page 22*

Topstitch, *page 23*

PREPARATION
- Cut **two** pieces of **outer tote fabric** 16" x 16"/40.5cm.

- Cut **two** pieces of **lining fabric** 16" x 16"/40.5cm.

- Cut **one** piece of **pocket fabric** 11" x 6¹/₂"/ 28 x 16.5cm.

- Cut **two** pieces of **strapping** 51"/129.5cm long.

- Cut **one** piece of **plastic or cardboard** 3³/₄" x 10³/₄"/9.5 x 27.5cm.

- Cut 2"/5cm squares out of each bottom corner of fabric and lining pieces.

CONSTRUCTION
OUTER TOTE

1 **Press top edge** ¹/₂"/1.3cm to the wrong side of each fabric piece.

2 **Mark two vertical lines** 4"/10cm from each side. Place the outside edge of the strap on each marking and stitch in place.

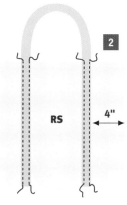

3 **With right sides together,** sew the tote together at the side seams and along the bottom, leaving the top seam allowance open and the 2"/5cm corners open. Press seams open.

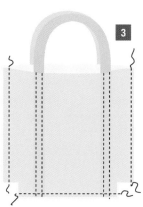

4 **Match the bottom seam** to the side seam and sew the corner seams.

RS

WS

5

5 **Turn tote to the outside.** Place the plastic or cardboard piece in the bottom. Stitch a few stitches through the bottom seam to secure in place.

POCKET AND LINING

6 **Sew** a 1"/2.5cm finished hem in the pocket top.

7 **Press** ½"/1.3cm seam allowances of the pocket sides and bottom to the wrong side.

8 **Center the pocket** 2"/5cm from the top of one lining piece and topstitch in place. Stitch a vertical line 3½"/9cm from one edge.

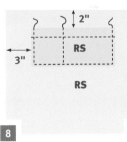

2"

RS

3"

RS

8

9 **Construct the lining pieces** same as for the outer tote.

10 **Insert the lining into the tote.** Pin the top edges together and topstitch. ✳

oversized carryall

This workhorse-of-a-bag is perfect for carrying large, heavy items like books, groceries, and gym gear.

FINISHED SIZE
17"/43cm wide x
18"/45.5cm high x
9"/23cm deep

MATERIALS
- 1½yd/1.5m fabric
- Two 16½"/42cm lengths of ⅜"/10mm wood dowel rods
- One 8" x 17"/ 20.5 x 43cm piece of foam board
- Chalk marker

TECHNIQUES
Finishing, *page 42*

Topstitch, *page 23*

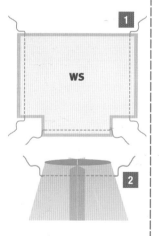

PREPARATION
- Cut **two** pieces of **fabric** 27"/68.5cm wide x 28½"/72.5cm high.

- Cut 4"/10cm squares out of the bottom corners of each rectangle.

CONSTRUCTION

1 **With right sides together,** stitch the sides and bottom of the bag, leaving the corner squares open. Press the seam open.

2 **With right sides together,** match the bottom seam with the side seam at each corner, matching the raw edges, and stitch.

3 **Finish the top edge** of the bag. Fold the top 5½"/14cm to the right side.

4 **Mark** 5"/12.5cm wide x 4"/10cm high handle openings in the center front and back of the bag. Starting 2"/5cm from the top fold, stitch along the marked lines. Trim, leaving ½"/1.3cm seam allowances. Clip to the corners.

5 **Mark the side openings** 2½"/6.5cm down from the top and 8"/20.5cm wide (4"/10cm from each side seam). Stitch along marked lines. Trim, leaving ½"/1.3cm seam allowances. Clip to the corners.

6 **Turn the facing** to the inside of the bag and press.

7 **Topstitch as shown,** leaving openings for the handles.

8 **Insert the dowel rods** into each top opening. Insert foam board into bottom of bag. ✳

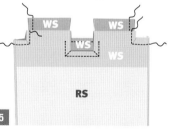

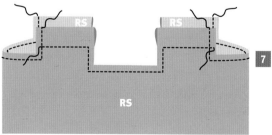

retro bucket bag

Shaped like a bucket, this lined bag is made from one pattern piece.
Old-fashioned rickrack trims the edges for a fun retro look.

FINISHED SIZE
16½"/42cm wide x
21"/53.5cm high

MATERIALS
- 1yd/1m fabric for bag
- 1yd/1m lining fabric
- One package rickrack trim
- One ⁷/₈"/22mm button
- 1yd/1m fusible web
- Pattern paper

TECHNIQUES
Adding
buttonholes, *page 30*

Edgestitch, *page 22*

Enlarging
a pattern, *page 16*

Lining (see On
the Inside), *page 14*

PREPARATION
- Using the **template grid** (at right), enlarge the drawing to make paper pattern.

- Using the paper pattern, cut out **two** pieces of **fabric** for the bag and **two** pieces of **lining**.

- Cut off top 2½"/6.5cm of **one bag handle** and **one lining handle** to use as the bag front.

- Trace the shape of the curved edges onto pattern paper. Draw a parallel line 1"/2.5cm from the first line.

- Cut a paper pattern.

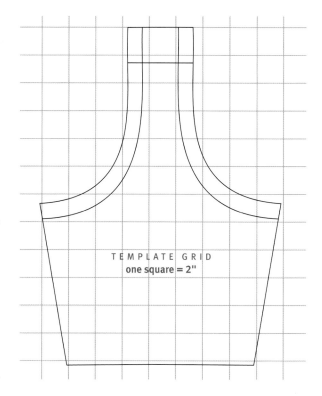

TEMPLATE GRID
one square = 2"

- Fuse a piece of fusible web to the wrong side of enough **lining fabric** to cut out **two** curved strips.

- Using the curved-strip paper pattern, cut out **two** fabric strips.

CONSTRUCTION

1 **Remove the paper backing** from the curved strips. Fuse the strips to the right side of each curved edge of the bag front and back.

iron

RS

2 **Lay rickrack to cover the raw edges** of the curved strips and stitch in place.

RS

retro bucket bag

3 **Fold the bottom corners** of the bag front and back to the right side, matching the two adjacent raw edges and creating a diagonal fold. Place a pin perpendicular to the raw edges 1"/2.5cm from the corner point.

4 **With right sides together,** pin the bag front to the back. Fold the bottom triangles opposite from one another at each corner. Stitch the sides and bottom of the bag together. Press the side seams open.

5 **With right sides together,** sew the lining front and back together at the side seams only.

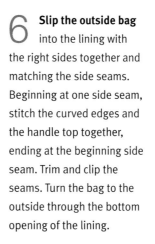

3

RS

WS

6 **Slip the outside bag** into the lining with the right sides together and matching the side seams. Beginning at one side seam, stitch the curved edges and the handle top together, ending at the beginning side seam. Trim and clip the seams. Turn the bag to the outside through the bottom opening of the lining.

7 **Keeping the bottom seam allowances** of the lining to the wrong side, edgestitch the bottom closed.

8 **Sew a buttonhole** on the longer handle end. Sew button on the shorter handle end to correspond to the buttonhole. ✳

suede hobo

This fashionable bag is made of asymmetrical pieces of felled wool and real suede that are sewn in an overlapping free-form design to a flower-motif lining.

FINISHED SIZE
19"/48cm wide x 15"/38cm high (excluding handles)

MATERIALS
- ¼yd/.25m each of five fabrics such as wool, felt or washed wool jersey
- One suede skin or pieces
- 2yd/2m lining fabric
- Pattern paper
- One pair 9"/23cm diameter wood handles

TECHNIQUES
Enlarging a pattern, *page 16*

Finishing, *page 42*

Lining (see On the Inside), *page 14*

Slipstitch, *page 24*

Topstitch, *page 23*

Walking foot (see Presser Feet), *page 21*

PREPARATION
- Using the **template grid** (see below), enlarge the pattern and draw the bag shape on pattern paper.

- Draw shapes of **fabric pieces** on pattern paper.

- Cut out each shape in various fabrics, adding extra fabric where necessary for underlapping. (If using suede, let the edge of the skin dictate the general character of the shapes and arrangements.)

- Using the bag pattern, cut out **two** pieces of **lining.**

- Cut **two** strips of **lining fabric** the width of the top of the bag plus seam allowances x 4"/10cm.

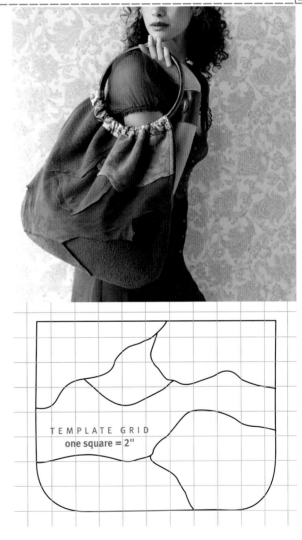

TEMPLATE GRID
one square = 2"

suede hobo

CONSTRUCTION

1 Lay each fabric piece on the wrong side of each lining piece, overlapping and arranging as desired. Topstitch all edges to the ground fabric (lining).

2 With right sides together, sew the bag front and back together leaving each side of the bag open 6"/15cm from the top. Finish the raw edges.

3 With right sides together, sew one casing strip to each top edge. Press the seam toward the casing.

4 Press the open side edges to the wrong side ½"/1.3cm. Topstitch.

5 Press the top edge of the casing to the wrong side ½"/1.3cm. Place a wood handle on the wrong side of each casing and fold the casing over the handle, matching the folded edge of the casing to the stitching line. Slipstitch or topstitch in place. ✳

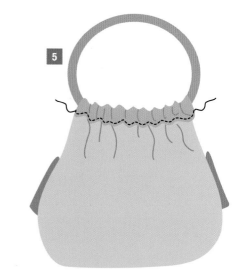

swing satchel

This no-frills carryall expands to hold just about everything, from clothes to books. Make it in a fun print fabric that's machine-washable.

FINISHED SIZE
20"/51cm wide x
17"/43cm high
(excluding handle)

MATERIALS
- 1½yd/1.5m fabric
- Safety pin
- Pattern paper

TECHNIQUES
Baste, *page 22*

Continuous
drawstring, *page 36*

Edgestitch, *page 22*

Enlarging
a pattern, *page 16*

Finishing, *page 42*

Staystitch, *page 23*

Topstitch, *page 23*

PREPARATION
- Cut **one** piece **fabric** 42"/106.5cm wide x 18½"/47cm high for the bag.

- Cut **one** piece **fabric** 2½" x 43"/6.5 x 109cm for the top facing.

- Cut **one** 8½"/21.5cm diameter circle for the bottom.

- Using the template grid, enlarge the pattern and cut **four** pieces **fabric** for the straps.

- Cut enough 1¼"/3cm wide strips to make **one** 54"/137cm long piece for the drawstring.

- Sew strips together if necessary.

TEMPLATE
GRID
one square = 2"

CONSTRUCTION

1 **Fold the bag in half** crosswise with right sides together and sew the side seam. Finish the seam together.

2 **Pin** ½"/1.3cm deep pleats about 1½"/4cm apart along the bottom edge of the bag. Staystitch along the seamline, holding the pleats in place.

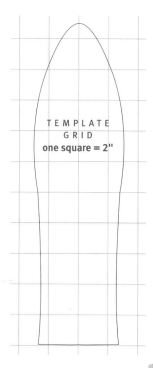

3 **Clip the bottom edge** every ¹⁄₂"/1.3cm to the staystitching.

4 **With right sides together,** pin the bag to the bottom circle, matching the raw edges and allowing the clipped seam allowance to spread open.

5 **Stitch** over the previous staystitching line. Finish the raw edges together.

4

swing satchel

6 **With right sides together,** sew two strap pieces together, leaving the short, straight ends open. Trim the seam allowance, turn to the right side and press. Edgestitch around the seamed edges. Repeat for the second strap.

7 **Lay the bag flat** with the side seam at the right. Measure and mark a center point of the bag front and back. With right sides together and matching raw edges, pin the center of one strap to the front marking and one strap to the back marking. Baste in place.

8 **Press the seam allowance** of one long edge of the top facing to the wrong side. Press the short ends to the wrong side. With right sides together, sew the unpressed edge of the facing to the top of the bag, sandwiching the straps.

9 **Trim the seam allowance** and turn the facing to the wrong side of the bag. Pin in place and topstitch along the loose edge, forming a casing.

10 **Make a drawstring.** Using the safety pin, insert the drawstring through the casing. Finish using the continuous drawstring method.

11 **Knot the straps** together as shown. ✳

roomy backpack

This versatile backpack is easy to make in any fabric, from industrial-strength nylon for hiking in the country to linen stripes for strolling in the city.

FINISHED SIZE
13½"/34cm wide x
15½"/39.5cm high x
5"/12.5cm deep
(excluding straps)

MATERIALS
- 1½yd/1.5m
  fabric for bag

- 1yd/1m fabric for lining

- One ¹³/₁₆"/31cm
  swivel ring

- Two pair ¹³/₁₆"/31cm
  D-rings

- Safety pin

TECHNIQUES
Adding
buttonholes, *page 30*

Baste, *page 22*

Drawstring, *page 35*

Edgestitch, *page 22*

Finishing, *page 42*

Lining (see On
the Inside), *page 14*

Pocket, *page 36*

Folded strap, *page 35*

Topstitch, *page 23*

PREPARATION
- Cut **one** piece **fabric**
15" x 38½"/38 x 97.5cm for
the bag.

- Cut **two** pieces **fabric**
6" x 17¼"/15 x 44cm for
the sides.

- Cut **one** piece **fabric**
14" x 11½"/35.5 x 29cm for
the flap.

- Cut **one** piece **fabric**
2" x 54"/5 x 137cm for the
drawstring. Cut two pieces
fabric 3½" x 6½"/
9 x 16.5cm for the short
straps.

- Cut **two** pieces **fabric**
3½" x 27"/9 x 68.5cm for
the long straps.

- Cut **one** piece **fabric**
2¼" x 3"/5.5 x 7.5cm for
the swivel ring loop.

- Cut **one** piece **fabric**
1" x 4"/2.5 x 10cm for the
loop closure.

- Cut **one** piece **lining**
15" x 38½"/38 x 97.5cm for
the front/bottom/back.

- Cut **two** pieces **lining**
6" x 17½"/15 x 44cm for
the sides.

- Cut **one** piece **lining**
14" x 11½"/35.5 x 29cm for
the flap.

- Cut **one** piece **lining**
15" x 10"/38 x 25.5cm for
the pocket.

roomy backpack

CONSTRUCTION

1 **Make pocket.** Pin finished top of pocket 6³/₄"/17cm down from the top edge of the bag lining. Edgestitch the sides and bottom. Stitch a vertical dividing line down the center of the pocket.

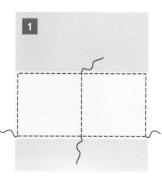

2 **With wrong sides together,** baste lining pieces to the bag and to the side pieces.

3 **Fold** ¹/₂"/1.3cm to the wrong side on one end of each strap piece. Make two short and two long 1¹/₄"/3cm wide straps with one finished end each.

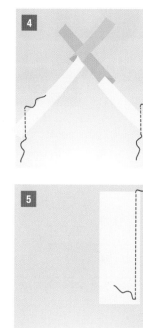

4 **With right sides together,** pin each long strap on the right side of the bag back, 12"/30.5cm below the top at a 45° angle along the edges of the bag. Baste along the seamline.

5 **With right sides together** and starting at one top front edge, stitch one side to the bag. Stop at the first corner ¹/₂"/1.3cm from the bottom raw edge. Insert the needle, clip the bag fabric to the needle and pivot the bag. Continue sewing along the bottom to the next corner. Clip the bag fabric to the needle and pivot again. Complete the side insertion. Trim seam to ¹/₄"/.6cm. Repeat for the other side.

6 **On the right side of the bag,** topstitch the sides and bottom seam, enclosing the raw edges. Stop stitching ¹/₄"/.6cm from the bottom corners. Sew the sides first and then the bottom seam.

7 **Mark buttonhole placements** 1"/2.5cm on both sides of center front and 1¹/₄"/3cm from the top of the bag. Stitch ¹/₂"/1.3cm buttonholes.

8 **Finish top of bag.** Turn 1¹/₄"/3cm to the wrong side and topstitch 1"/2.5cm from the top folded edge.

9 **Make one** 54"/137cm drawstring. Using the safety pin, feed through one buttonhole and through the casing and out the other buttonhole. Knot both ends.

roomy backpack

10 **Pin raw edges of** the short straps to the top edge of the back of the bag, placing them 3$\frac{1}{2}$"/9cm from each side. Baste in place.

11 **Press** $\frac{1}{2}$"/1.3cm to the wrong side on each side of the swivel ring loop piece. Feed the loop through the swivel ring. Pin the loop to the right side of the bottom center of the flap, matching all raw edges. Baste in place.

12 **With right sides together,** sew the flap to the flap lining, leaving the top open. Trim the seam and turn to the outside. Topstitch.

13 **Center the right side** of the flap 1$\frac{1}{4}$"/3cm below the top of the back. Stitch a $\frac{1}{2}$"/1.3cm seam, then trim to $\frac{1}{4}$"/.6cm. Fold the flap over the seam allowance and topstitch to cover the raw edge.

14 **Fold the loop closure piece** in half. Then fold the raw edges to the center fold and edgestitch. Fold in half crosswise. Sew to the front of the bag to correspond with the swivel ring. Fold back on itself, covering the raw edge and stitch again.

15 **Feed the ends of** the short straps through two D-rings. Topstitch. Loop the long straps through the D-rings. Adjust to desired length. ✳

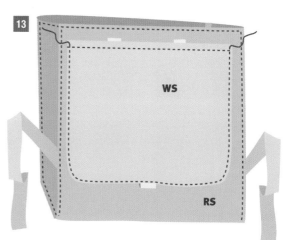

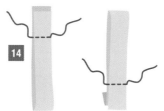

courier bag

This totally hip, yet functional, bag can be worn long or short by adjusting the shoulder strap. It sports fun contrasting fabric in just the right places.

FINISHED SIZE

15"/38cm wide x
15"/38cm high
(excluding shoulder strap)

MATERIALS

- 5/8yd/.6m fabric for bag

- 1/4yd/.25m contrasting fabric for bottom, facing and strap closure

- 2"/50mm-wide quick-release buckle

- Two 1 1/2"/38mm-wide single bar slides

- 1 1/2yd/1.5m of 1 1/2"/38mm-wide webbing

TECHNIQUES

Edgestitch, *page 22*

Enlarging
a pattern, *page 16*

Fabric tube, *page 34*

Staystitch, *page 23*

Topstitch, *page 23*

PREPARATION

- Using the **template grid** (see page 91), enlarge the design to make a paper pattern for the bag bottom.

- Cut **one** piece **fabric** 37"/94cm wide x 19"/48cm high for the bag.

- Using the bottom pattern piece, cut **one** bottom piece in **contrasting fabric.**

- Cut **one** piece **contrasting fabric** 5" x 14"/12.5 x 35.5cm for upper front closure strap.

- Cut **one** piece **contrasting fabric** 5" x 22"/12.5 x 56cm for lower front closure strap.

- Cut **one** piece **contrasting fabric** 2" x 37"/5 x 94cm for the top facing.

- Cut **one** piece **webbing** 48"/122cm long.

- Cut **one** piece **webbing** 8"/20.5cm long.

- Cut **two** strips of **lining fabric** the width of the top of the bag plus seam allowances x 4"/10cm.

courier bag

CONSTRUCTION

1 **With right sides together,** sew short sides of the bag piece together. Press seam open.

2 **Staystitch the bottom edge** of the bag along the seamline. Clip every $\frac{1}{2}$"/1.3cm to the stitching line.

3 **Using the two contrasting fabric strips,** make two fabric tubes 2"/5cm wide for the upper and lower front closure straps.

4 **Insert the lower front closure strap** through the bottom portion of the quick-release buckle. Fold the strap in half.

5 **Center the folded strap** on the front of the bag, aligning the raw edges with the bottom edge of the bag. Edgestitch the bottom edge of the strap to the bag.

6 **With right sides together,** sew the bag to the bottom, letting the clips spread around the curves.

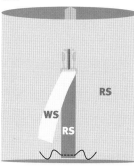

7 **Press one long edge** of the contrasting top facing piece $\frac{1}{2}$"/1.3cm to the wrong side. Sew the two short ends together with right sides together. Press open.

8 **With right sides together,** sew the unpressed edge of the facing to the top of the bag opening. Trim the seam. Fold the facing to the wrong side of the bag and topstitch in place.

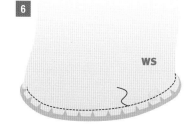

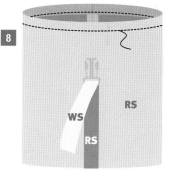

courier bag

9 **Insert the upper front closure strap** through the top portion of the quick-release buckle. Fold in half, then fold the ends ½"/1.3cm to the wrong side to finish; press. Sandwich the top edge of the back of the bag between the strap ends, centering the strap over the back seam so fold at buckle is 1"/2.5cm from top edge of bag. Edgestitch the strap, sewing through all layers.

10 **Allow the bag to lie flat** and mark the "side edges." Turn one end of shorter piece of webbing 1"/2.5cm to the wrong side; press. Insert opposite end of webbing through one single slide bar. Turn opposite end of webbing over to the wrong side so short ends meet. Pin webbing to the back side of the bag about ½"/1.3cm from the right "side edge" and 3½"/9cm from the top edge. Topstitch a rectangle to attach the strap to the bag. Reinforce by sewing an "X" through the square.

11 **Turn one end** of longer piece of webbing 1"/2.5cm to the wrong side; press. Pin the longer piece of webbing to the other side of the bag back. Topstitch and reinforce.

12 **Feed the longer webbing** through the second slide bar, through the shorter webbing slide bar, then back through the second slide bar. Turn the end of the longer webbing ½"/1.3cm to the wrong side twice and topstitch. Adjust the strap length as desired. ✳

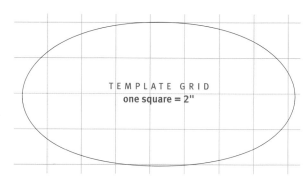

TEMPLATE GRID
one square = 2"

drawstring pouch

This little bag has four identical sides and uses ribbon for loops and handle. The pocket is embroidered with Japanese *sashiko* (see page 96), here using variegated floss.

FINISHED SIZE

7½"/19cm wide x
11"/28cm high x
7½"/19cm deep
(excluding handle)

MATERIALS

- ½yd/.5m fabric for bag
- ½yd/.5m underlining fabric for bag
- ¼yd/.25m contrast fabric for front panel
- ½yd/.5m lining
- 2yd/2m of ⅜"/10mm-wide ribbon
- One ⅝"/16mm button
- Pattern paper

TECHNIQUES

Baste, *page 22*

Enlarging
a pattern, *page 16*

Lining, underlining (see
On the Inside), *page 14*

Prairie points, *page 38*

Running stitch, *page 24*

Sewing on
a button, *page 43*

Slipstitch, *page 24*

Topstitch, *page 23*

PREPARATION

- Using the **template grid** (see page 96), enlarge the drawing to make the paper pattern.

- Cut **four** bag pieces in **bag fabric**.

- Cut **four** bag pieces in **lining fabric**.

- Cut **four** bag pieces in **underlining**.

- Cut **one** front panel piece in **contrasting fabric**.

- Cut **one** front panel piece in **lining fabric**.

- Cut **one** front panel in **underlining**.

- Cut **one** piece of **ribbon** 48"/122cm for the handle.

- Cut **one** piece of **ribbon** 3"/7.5cm for the button loop.

- Cut **eight** pieces of **ribbon** 2"/5cm long for the handle loops.

- **Baste** the underlining fabric pieces to four bag pieces and one front panel. (It is not necessary to underline the front panel if you are sewing the **sashiko technique** to the front panel.)

drawstring pouch

CONSTRUCTION

1 **Make one ribbon prairie point** (see page 38). Center the prairie point on the right side of the top edge of the front panel. Baste in place.

2 **With right sides together,** sew the corresponding lining piece to the front panel along the top edge. Trim the seam, press open first, then press the lining to the wrong side. Topstitch along the top edge.

3 **Place the lining side** of the front panel on one bag piece. Baste around the sides. Sew a button to the bag front to correspond with the prairie point button loop.

4 **With right sides together,** sew the bag front to one bag piece, starting and stopping the stitching ½"/1.3cm from the top edge and the bottom point.

5 **Continue sewing** the bag pieces together, always starting and stopping the stitching ½"/1.3cm from the top edge and the bottom point. Trim the seams and press open.

6 **Repeat steps 4 and 5** to construct the bag lining, leaving an opening along one seam for turning.

7 **Fold** each 2"/5cm piece of ribbon in half lengthwise, then stitch edges together along the length.

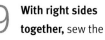
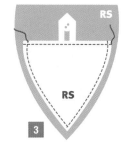

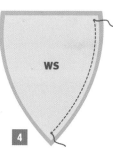

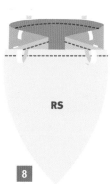

8 **Fold each ribbon piece** in half to form a loop and place two loops on each bag section, each 1½"/4cm from a seam. Baste in place.

9 **With right sides together,** sew the lining to the bag along the top edge. Trim the seam and turn the bag to the outside through the lining opening. Press the top edge, then topstitch. Slipstitch the opening closed.

10 **Thread the ribbon** for the handle through the loops. Sew the ribbon ends together to make a continuous handle.

drawstring pouch

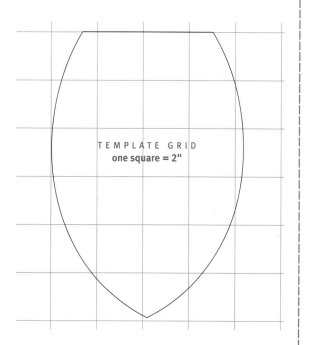

TEMPLATE GRID
one square = 2"

✂ SASHIKO TECHNIQUE

A Japanese embroidery technique called *sashiko* has been used to embellish the front panel. If using this optional step in the bag-making, the following **additional materials** are needed:

- ¹⁄₄yd/.25m cotton flannel
- One skein six-strand cotton embroidery floss
- Crewel embroidery needle
- Plastic quilt pattern template

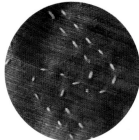

- **Underline** the front panel with cotton flannel.

- **Using a quilt template,** trace a design with pencil on the flannel side of the front panel.

- **Thread a crewel embroidery needle** with three strands of embroidery floss.

- **Working from the flannel side** of the piece, hand sew even running stitches along the pencil lines.

- **Knot the threads** at the end of each thread tail. ✳

**NEED TO SPICE UP
YOUR WARDROBE**
without spending a bundle?
Check out this chapter's twelve
quick and easy projects for
fun fashions and accessories like
scarves, a belt, and a brooch,
plus a tube top and a skirt.

wear it

sheer geometry scarf

Shimmering little squares with peek-a-boo holes adorn this airy sheer scarf.
Follow this design or make your own glittery shapes in monotone or contrasting colors.

SIZE
8" x 58"/20.5 x 147.5cm

MATERIALS
- 1⅝yd/1.5m of sheer fabric
- ⅛yd/.2m pieces of taffeta, satin or charmeuse fabric for square accents
- Fusible web
- Buttonhole cutter and wood block

TECHNIQUES
Finishing, *page 42*

Hemmer foot (see Presser Feet), *page 21*

PREPARATION
- Cut or tear **one** piece of **sheer fabric** 8" x 58"/20.5 x 147.5cm.

- Following the manufacturer's instructions, fuse web to the wrong side of the accent fabrics.

- Cut **forty** 1½"/4cm **accent** squares.

CONSTRUCTION

1 **Remove the paper backing** from the small squares. Place five squares along one short end of the scarf, matching the edges of each square with the raw edge of the scarf and spacing them about ½"/1.3cm apart. Fuse the squares to the scarf.

2 **Repeat another row** of five squares next to the previous row and fuse in place.

3 **Continue fusing squares** with a row of four squares, three squares, two squares and finishing with one square.

4 **Repeat this pattern** at the opposite end of the scarf.

5 **Using the buttonhole cutter** and a block of wood, cut a random pattern of square holes through a few of the fused squares.

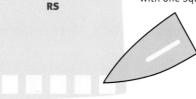

RS

6

6 **Trim the sheer fabric** between each end square to make a "fringe."

7 **Finish the long edges** of the sheer scarf. ✳

pearl essence belt

Dyed pearl buttons embellish the ends of this narrow belt of tone-on-tone fabric. Each button is hand-tied, which adds interesting fringed texture to the back side of the project.

FINISHED SIZE
4" x 54"/10 x 137cm

MATERIALS
- ½yd/.25m of fabric for scarf
- ½yd/.25m of fabric for lining
- Sixty-two pearl-finish buttons in various colors
- Twine or embroidery floss
- Crewel embroidery needle

TECHNIQUES
Seams
(see Pressing), *page 30*

Slipstitch, *page 24*

Trimming seams and corners, *page 28*

PREPARATION
- Cut **one** piece of **fabric** 5" x 54"/12.5 x 137cm. If your fabric is not 54"/137cm wide, cut two pieces and sew them together in the center or insert a transition contrasting section to connect them.

- Cut **one** piece of **lining fabric** 5" x 54"/12.5 x 137cm.

- Cut a 45° angle at each end of both the scarf and lining pieces.

CONSTRUCTION

1 **With right sides together,** sew the scarf and lining together leaving an opening along one side. Trim the seams and corners and turn to the outside. Slipstitch the opening closed.

2 **Thread the crewel embroidery needle** with a length of twine or embroidery floss. Sew one button at the point of each end, taking one stitch from back to front and again to the back side. Knot the thread and trim the thread ends.

3 **Repeat consecutive rows** of buttons until thirty-one buttons have been sewn to each end. ✳

confetti fleece scarf

This soft and cuddly, extra-long fleece scarf is easy to make and easy to wear. Accent it with a generous sprinkling of confetti-like squares.

SIZE
8½" x 88"/21.5 x 223.5cm

MATERIALS
- ¼yd/.25m each of four colors of fleece

TECHNIQUES
Bar tack, *page 22*

Edgestitch, *page 22*

1	2	3	4	3	2	1

PREPARATION
- Cut **two** pieces of **color 1** fleece 9" x 19"/23 x 48cm.

- Cut **two** pieces of **color 2** fleece 9" x 12½"/ 23 x 31cm.

- Cut **two** pieces of **color 3** fleece 9" x 9"/23 x 23cm.

- Cut **one** piece of **color 4** fleece 9" x 15"/23 x 38cm.

- Cut approximately **120** squares of fleece in mixed colors.

RS

✂ TIP
The squares can be hand-tacked in place as well. Use a heavy cord or yarn and leave long ends for added texture.

CONSTRUCTION

1 **Starting at one end,** lay the fleece pieces overlapping one another about ½"/1.3cm in the following order: color 1, color 2, color 3, color 4, color 3, color 2 and color 1.

2 **Sew a double row** of stitching to connect each section.

3 **To even the edges,** lay the scarf on a flat surface and re-cut the long edges.

4 **Sprinkle the squares** on top of the scarf, concentrating them at each end. Pin in place.

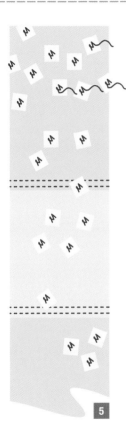

5 **Bar tack** each
square in place. ✳

fabric brooch

This delightful fabric flower adds a dash of fashion flair. Choose three or more fabrics of contrasting weights and textures to achieve the same look.

FINISHED SIZE

Approximately 5"/12.7cm in diameter

MATERIALS

- ¼yd/.25m pieces of 3 or 4 fabrics
- Small button
- Polyester thread
- Pin back
- Pattern paper

PREPARATION

- Enlarge patterns 150%; make paper patterns for petals **A**, **B** and **C.**

- Cut **two** or **three** pieces of each fabric using patterns **A**, **B** and **C.**

CONSTRUCTION

1 **Knot one end of the thread** and sew a running stitch by hand through the center of each petal.

2 **Pull the thread** to gather the center of each petal and knot the thread to secure the gathers.

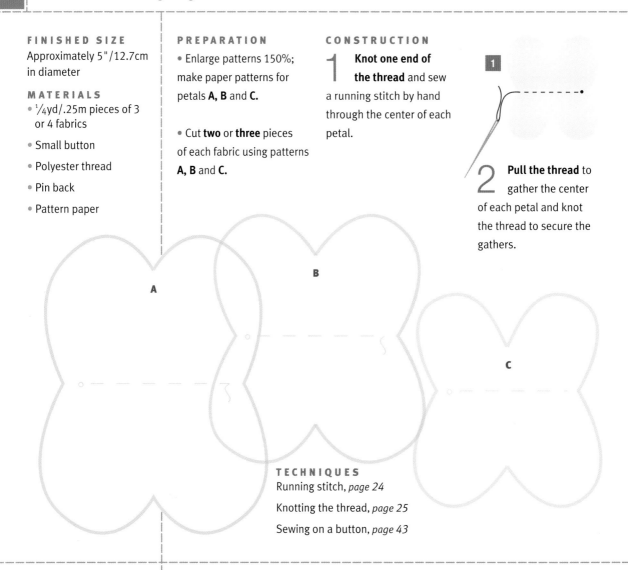

TECHNIQUES

Running stitch, *page 24*

Knotting the thread, *page 25*

Sewing on a button, *page 43*

A

B

C

3 **Stack the petals** in a pleasing arrangement, beginning with size A and ending with size C. Hand-sew them together in the center.

4 **Snip and tear the edges** of the petals to shred them, removing a few threads.

5 **Sew a few loose threads** to the center of the flower. Sew a button in the center.

6 **Sew on** pin back. ✳

5

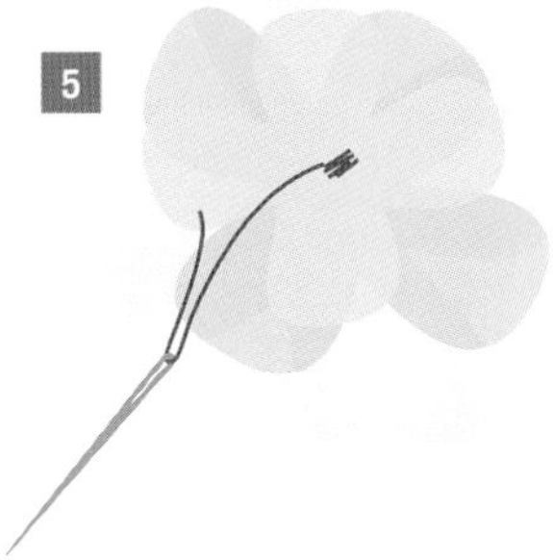

gossamer ribbon scarf

Rows of twisted and sheer ribbons are sewn "on air" to create this light and whimsical scarf.
Use one type of ribbon, or mix in a few novelty yarns for your own unique design.

FINISHED SIZE

Approximately
6" x 90"/15 x 228.5cm

MATERIALS

• 50 to 60yd/46 to 55m of ribbon

• Water soluble stabilizer

• Sponge

• Rayon or polyester decorative sewing thread

TECHNIQUES

Backstitch, *page 22*

Fusing, *page 41*

PREPARATION

• Cut **eighteen** to **twenty-four** (depending on the ribbon width) strands **ribbon** 90"/228.5cm long

• Cut **fourteen** pieces of water soluble **stabilizer** 6" x 10"/15 x 25.5cm

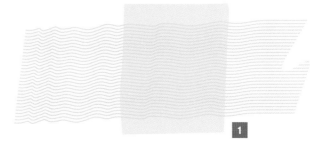

CONSTRUCTION

1 **Place one piece of stabilizer** on a flat surface. Moisten the surface with a sponge. Starting about 13"/33cm from the ends of the ribbons, lay eighteen to twenty-four strands of ribbon parallel to one another and centered on the stabilizer. Finger press them to stick to the stabilizer.

2 **Lay another piece of stabilizer** on top of the ribbons and finger press to the under layer stabilizer.

3 **Stitch ten to twelve parallel lines** of stitching ½"/1.3cm apart through all layers. Backstitch at the beginning and end of the stitching.

4 **Repeat steps 1 through 3** six or seven more times, leaving about 6"/15cm between stitch groups and about 13"/33cm of ribbon fringe at the opposite of the scarf.

5 **Following the manufacturer's instructions,** soak the scarf in water to remove the stabilizer. Allow to dry. Trim the fringe ends as desired. ✳

✂ TIPS

- *Use the gridlines on a cutting mat to line up the ribbons perfectly even.*
- *If you want a fuller look, randomly tie shorter strands of ribbon to the scarf.*

tablet tote

Designed to hold just your tablet or eReader and a few essentials, this little tote is made to sling over your shoulder. Add trim to the bottom seam and "tag" it as yours.

FINISHED SIZE
7"/17.5cm wide x 9"/23cm high (excluding strap)

MATERIALS
- ½yd/.5m fabric for bag
- ½yd/.25m lining fabric
- ½yd/.25m fringed selvage
- ⅓yd/.3m of ⅝"/16mm ribbon
- Scrap of fusible web

TECHNIQUES
Baste, *page 22*

Edgestitch, *page 22*

Folded strap, *page 35*

Lining (see On the Inside), *page 14*

Selvage (see Fabric Basics), *page 12*

Trimming seams and corners, *page 28*

PREPARATION
- Cut **two** pieces fabric 8" x 10"/20.5 x 25.5cm for the bag.

- Cut **two** pieces **fabric** 8" x 10"/20.5 x 25.5cm for the lining.

- Cut **one** piece **fabric** 1¾" x 49"/4.5 x 124.5cm for strap.

- Cut **one** piece **fabric selvage** 8"/20.5cm wide— add seam allowance to fringed edge.

- Cut **one** piece **ribbon** 7"/17.5cm long for the bottom trim.

- Cut **one** piece **ribbon** 3"/7.5cm long for the tag.

CONSTRUCTION

1 **Using a strip of fusible web,** fuse 7"/17.5cm piece of ribbon to the right side of the fringed selvage. Fold the ribbon ends on a 45° angle to miter and finish the ends.

2 **With right sides together** and matching raw edges, baste the fringed selvage to the bottom of one bag piece along the seamline.

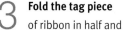

3 **Fold the tag piece** of ribbon in half and place 2"/5cm from the top left on the right side of the fabric bag with the loop toward the center of the bag.

4 **With right sides together,** sew the sides and bottom of the bag together. Trim the corners. Press the seam open and turn to the outside.

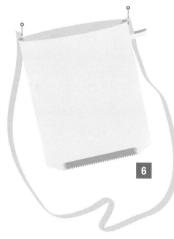

5 **Make one** 49"/124.5cm long fabric strap.

6 **Matching raw edges,** pin strap to right side of each side seam.

7 **With right sides together,** sew the lining together on three sides, leaving top edge open and leaving an opening on the bottom edge. Press seams open.

8 **Place the bag inside the lining** with the right sides together and sew around the top edge.

8

9 **Turn the bag to the outside** through the bottom opening of the lining. Fold the lining seam allowances to the wrong side and edgestitch the opening closed.

10 **Press** the top edge. ✳

sequin pocket scarf

Large glittery paillettes are cleverly cloaked
inside sewn pockets in this double-layer chiffon scarf.

FINISHED SIZE
6" x 45"/15 x 114.5cm

MATERIALS
- ¹/₂yd/.5m of sheer chiffon fabric
- Fifty 20mm silver hologram paillette sequins
- Pattern paper
- Temporary spray adhesive

TECHNIQUES
Slipstitch, *page 24*

Walking foot (see Presser Feet), *page 21*

✂ TIP

Using a walking foot or an even-feed foot prevents the fabric from shifting as you sew.

PREPARATION
- Tear or cut **two** pieces of **fabric** 7" x 45"/17.5 x 114.5cm

- Make **two** paper grid templates as follows: On each template, draw five ¹¹/₈"/2.8cm squares across and five down.

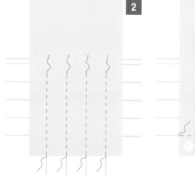

CONSTRUCTION

1 **With right sides together,** stitch the two scarf pieces together around all edges leaving an opening along one long edge. Trim the seams to ¹/₈"/.3cm. Turn to the outside and lightly press.

2 **Spray adhesive on each paper template.** Pin three edges of one end of the finished scarf over the gridlines on the paper template. Sew through the scarf and the paper, stitching the vertical lines first.

WS

3 **Insert one paillette** into each vertical opening through the side opening of the scarf. Stitch the first horizontal gridline through all layers.

4 **Insert another set of paillettes** into the vertical openings and sew another horizontal line. Repeat for all five grids.

5 **Repeat steps 3 and 4** at the other end of the scarf using the second paper template.

6 **Tear away the paper** from the back of the scarf. Slipstitch the scarf opening closed. ✳

tube top

Create a classic summer fashion from four simple strips of stretch-knit fabric.
A novel shoelace drawstring adjusts the fit and adds an unexpected touch of color.

SIZE

Preparation directions are for **X-Small.** Changes for **Small, Medium** and **Large** are explained. Please refer to measurement chart (see page 128) before you begin.

MATERIALS

- 1yd/1m of stretch-knit fabric
- Contrasting color shoelace
- ¼yd/.25m of ¼"/6mm wide elastic
- Large safety pin
- Polyester thread

TECHNIQUES

Backstitch, *page 22*

Double-stitched seam, *page 29*

Drawstring, *page 35*

Drawstring casing, *page 36*

Stitch in the ditch, *page 22*

PREPARATION

- Cut **two** pieces of **fabric** 15½"/39.5cm wide by 15"/38cm long for the body. To make a larger size, **add** 1"/2.5cm in width to each rectangle for every additional size. For example, the rectangle size for Medium should be 17½"/44.5cm wide by 15"/38cm long.

- Cut **two** pieces of **fabric** 4"/10cm wide by 30"/76cm long for the bands. To determine length for Medium, for example, subtract 1"/2.5cm from the width of the rectangle (16½"/42cm), multiply the number by 2 (33"/84cm), then add 1"/2.5cm; 34"/86.5cm.

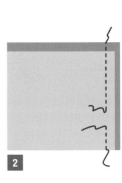

CONSTRUCTION

1 **With right sides together,** sew the side seams of the body pieces together. Use a double-stitched seam finish.

2 **With right sides together,** sew the short end of one band. For the second band, sew the seam for 2½"/6.5cm and backstitch. Skip ½"/1.3cm before starting to stitch again. Backstitch and continue sewing for 1"/2.5cm to the end. Press seams open.

3 **With right sides together,** pin one edge of the first band to the bottom edge of the body, placing the seam in the band at the center back. Stitch, stretching the band to fit the body as you sew.

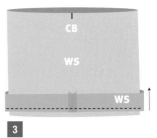

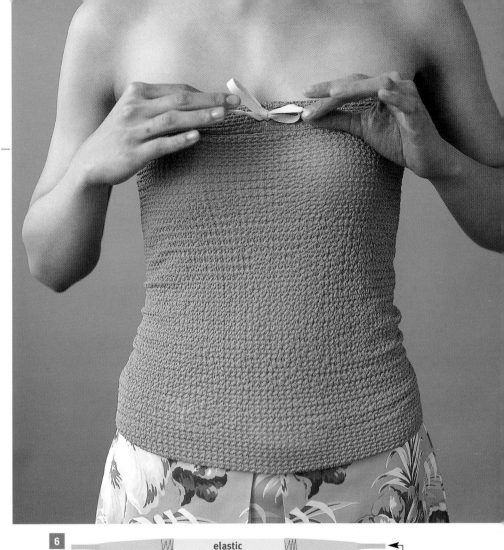

4 **Fold the band in half** with the wrong sides together, extending the raw edge ½"/1.3cm beyond the seamline. Pin frequently. From the top (right) side, stitch in the ditch through the seamline. Trim the excess fabric next to the stitching on the wrong side.

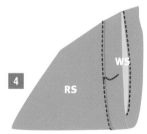

5 **Sew the second band** to the top of the tube, this time placing the ½"/1.3cm opening at the center front and nearest the raw edges. Stitch, stretching the band to fit the body as you sew. Repeat step 4 to finish the band.

6 **Cut the shoelace in half.** Stitch each end to the ends of the piece of elastic, adjusting the length of the elastic according to your size.

7 **Attach the safety pin** to one end of the shoelace and feed the shoelace, or drawstring, through the opening in the top band. ✳

scrap fabric boa

Different combinations of fabrics create endless possibilities for this faux-fabulous boa scarf. It's super-easy to make with only one row of stitching.

FINISHED SIZE
4" x 72"/10 x 183cm

MATERIALS
- ¼yd/.25m each of eight fabrics such as netting, crinkled organza, polyester prints and novelty weaves
- One pair dangling bead earrings

PREPARATION
- Cut **eight** pieces of **fabric** 4" x 72"/10 x 183cm. When using the pieces of fabric that are shorter than 72"/183cm, cut one more strip.

✄ **TIP**

Polyester and nylon fabrics work best for this scarf. Finely woven silk tends to disintegrate, but silk douppioni works well.

CONSTRUCTION

1 **Stack eight layers** of fabric on top of one another. Place multiple strips of the same fabric end to end. There is no need to sew them together. Pin all layers together.

2 **Sew a line of stitching** down the center of the strips through all layers

3 **Clip through all layers** from the raw edges to the center stitching line. Clip approximately ³/₄"/1.9cm apart.

4 **Wash and dry** the scarf to ravel and rag the edges.

5 **Clip on or sew** an earring to each end. ✳

wrap skirt

Made using two overlapping pieces of fabric that are stitched at an angle at the back to create an asymmetrical wrap at the front, this skirt is easy to adjust to fit your size.

SIZE
One size fits most

MATERIALS
- $1^2/_3$ yd/1.6m fabric
- Two 1"/25mm buttons
- Thread
- Manila file folder (tag board)

TECHNIQUES
Adding buttonholes, *page 30*

Sewing a hem, *page 32*

Sewing on a button, *page 43*

Topstitch, *page 23*

PREPARATION
- Cut **two** pieces of **fabric** 30" x $38^1/_2$"/76 x 97.5cm.

- Cut **one** piece **tag board** $1^3/_4$" x $11^1/_2$"/4.5 x 29cm.

- Cut **one** piece **tag board** $1^1/_4$" x $11^1/_2$"/3 x 29cm.

- Draw a line on one template $^1/_2$"/1.3cm from one long edge.

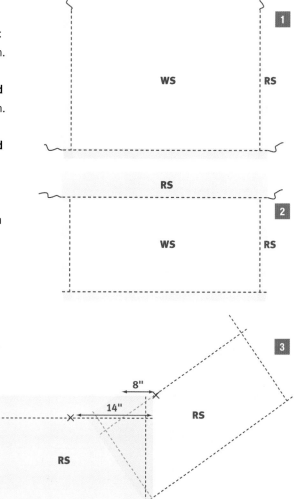

CONSTRUCTION

1 **Using the template method** of pressing hems, press 1¼"/3cm finished hems in the sides and bottom of each rectangle. Topstitch the side hems in place first, then topstitch the bottom hem.

2 **Using the template** with the ½"/1.3cm-marked line, press ½"/1.3cm to the wrong side of the top hem. Now, press the top hem 4"/10cm to the wrong side.

3 **Pin one rectangle** over the other rectangle according to the drawing. Wrap the skirt around yourself and adjust the angle and placement for size and fit.

4 **Follow the drawing** to topstitch along the previous hem seamlines.

5 **Make a buttonhole** in the upper corner of each rectangle.

6 **Try on the skirt** and mark the button placements. Sew on the buttons. ✳

RS

RS

4

connecting scarves

Two scarves, coordinating and reversible, join together with clever knotted buttons through multi-stitched buttonholes. Wear both as a long two-piece scarf, or just one for a shorter version.

SIZE

Each is 8" x 29" / 20.5 x 73.5cm

MATERIALS

- ¹⁄₂yd/.5m of two coordinating fabrics
- ¹⁄₈yd/.2m of accent fabric
- Decorative thread

TECHNIQUES

Baste, *page 30*

Knotted buttons, *page 37*

Seams (see Pressing), *page 41*

Slipstitch, *page 24*

Trimming seams and corners, *page 28*

PREPARATION

- Cut **two** pieces of each **coordinating fabric** 9" x 30"/23 x 76cm.

- Cut **four** strips of **accent fabric** 1½" x 20"/4 x 51cm for flat piping.

- Cut **four** strips of **accent fabric** 1³⁄₄" x 8½"/4.5 x 21.5cm for the button knots.

- Cut **two** 3"/7.5cm squares of **accent fabric** for buttonholes. Cut the squares in half diagonally to make four triangles.

CONSTRUCTION

1 **Fold each piping strip** in half lengthwise with the wrong sides together. Press.

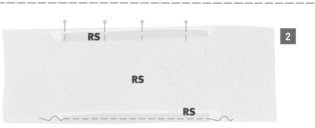

2 **Pin a piping strip** to the right side of each long edge of two scarf pieces. Center the strips with the folded edge towards the center. Fold each end of the piping diagonally to finish the strips. Baste in place.

3 **Make** four knotted buttons.

4 **On the right side** of each trimmed scarf piece and matching the raw edges, evenly space two knotted buttons across one short end. Each knot should be 2½"/6.5cm from each side. Baste in place.

5 **With right sides together,** sew the corresponding scarf pieces to the trimmed pieces, leaving an opening along one long edge. Trim the seams and corners and turn to the outside. Slipstitch the opening closed. Press.

connecting scarves

6 **Mark the placement** of two buttonholes on each scarf to correspond to the knotted buttons on the opposite end.

7 **Pin the right side** of two raw-edged triangles to either side of the plain end of each scarf.

8 **Stitching through all layers,** sew an almond-shaped outline large enough for the button knots to slip through. Clip through the center of the outline and to the ends of the almond shape. Pull the fabric triangle through the opening to the opposite side of the scarf. Press.

9 **Starting with a line of stitching** parallel to the opening, sew a concentric almond-shaped spiral around the opening until all of the triangle is sewn down. Press. ✳

buttonhole scarf

Fabric rectangles are stitched together to make openings that look like big bound buttonholes. Toss one end through the opening at the other end for a unique look.

FINISHED SIZE
6" x 46"/15 x 117cm

MATERIALS
- ³/₄yd/.75m of drape fabric for the scarf body and ends
- ¹/₄yd/.25m of accent fabric
- ¹/₈yd/.2m of fabric for "buttonhole" edges

TECHNIQUES
Seams
(see Pressing), *page 41*

Slipstitch, *page 24*

Trimming seams and corners, *page 28*

PREPARATION
- Cut **two** pieces of **scarf fabric** 29" x 7"/73.5 x 17.5cm for the scarf body.

- Cut **two** pieces of **scarf fabric** 7" x 7"/17.5 x 17.5cm for the scarf ends.

- Cut **four** pieces of **accent fabric** 6¹/₂" x 7"/16.5 x 17.5cm.

- Cut **four** strips of **buttonhole edge fabric** 1¹/₂" x 7"/4 x 17.5cm.

buttonhole scarf

CONSTRUCTION

1 **With right sides together,** stitch one long edge of a buttonhole edge strip to the 7"/17.5cm side of an accent piece.

2 **Sew the other long edge** to the accent piece to form a tube. Trim the seams to ¼"/.6cm and press the seams open. Make three more sections.

3 **With wrong sides together,** press the tubes in half lengthwise forming ¼"/.6cm trimmed edges.

4 **Position two accent tubes** on the right side of each end piece so that the ¼"/.6cm trimmed edges lie next to each other at the center. Stitch, trim and press the seam toward the end piece.

5 **Press the seam allowance** to the wrong side of each end piece.

6 **With right sides together,** fold the end piece in half crosswise. Stitch each side seam. Trim the corners.

7 **Turn the ends** to the right side and slip-stitch the opening. Press.

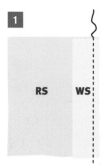

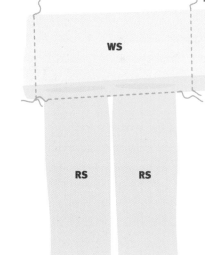

8 **Center each accent end** on the short ends of the scarf body. Stitch, trim the seams and press the seams toward the scarf body.

9 **Fold the corners of each end piece** to the center of the scarf and pin. With right sides together, sew the two scarf bodies together, leaving an opening along one long edge. Trim the corners and turn the scarf to the outside. Slipstitch the opening. ✳

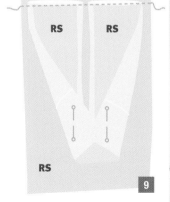

RS RS

RS

9

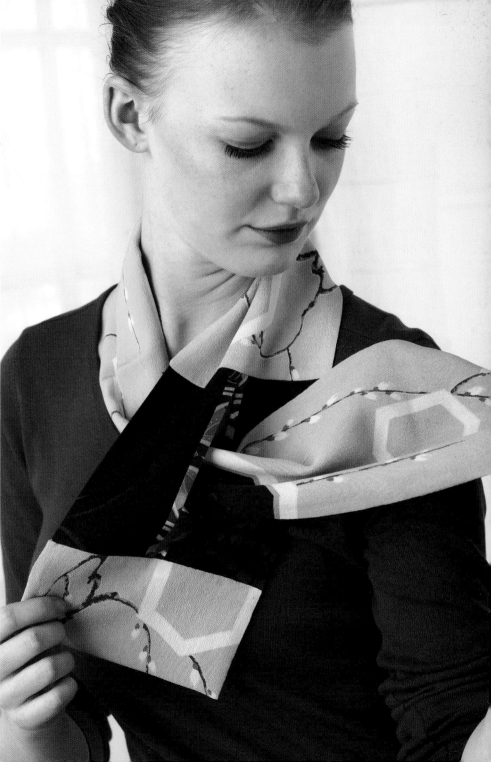

helpful information

helpful information

SOURCES

You can find all the materials, tools, and equipment you need to make the projects in this book—fabric, notions, sewing machines, and more—at your local crafts, sewing, or quilting retailer, as well as from various sources online. Feel free to substitute the fabrics and other items shown in the projects to give them your personal touch.

MEASUREMENT CHART
See the Tube Top project on page 114

SIZE	BUST	WAIST	HIPS
extra small	32"	24"	34"
small	34"	26"	36"
medium	36"	28"	38"
large	38"	30"	40"
extra large	42"	34"	44"